STRONGER
Than
STEEL

STRONGER
Than
STEEL

SPIDER SILK DNA AND THE QUEST FOR BETTER
BULLETPROOF VESTS, SUTURES, AND PARACHUTE ROPE

Bridget Heos

with photographs by Andy Comins

Houghton Mifflin Books for Children • Houghton Mifflin Harcourt • Boston   New York   2013

For my brother Luke, a doctor and researcher. —B.H.

For Nana. —A.C.

Library of Congress Cataloging-in-Publication Data:
Heos, Bridget. Stonger than steel/ Bridget Heos ; [illustrated by] Andy Comins.
p. cm. — (Scientists in the field series)
Summary: "In *Stronger Than Steel,* readers enter Randy Lewis' lab, where they come face to face with golden orb weaver spiders and transgenic alfalfa, silkworm silk, and goats, whose milk contains the proteins to spin spider silk—and to weave a nearly indestructible fiber. Learn how this amazing material might someday be used to repair or replace human ligaments and bones, improve body armor, strengthen parachute rope, and even tether an airplane to an aircraft carrier. Readers explore rapid advancements in the application of genetic medicine and their potential to save and improve lives while considering the crucial ethical concerns of genetic research. A timely addition to the acclaimed Scientists in the Field series." — Provided by publisher.
ISBN 978-0-547-68126-9 (hardback) 1. Nephila maculata—Juvenile literature. 2. Spider webs—Juvenile literature. 3. Spider webs—Therapeutic use—Juvenile literature. 4. Scientists—Juvenile literature. I. Comins, Andy, ill. II. Title.
QL458.42.T48H46 2013 595.4'4—dc23 2012010992

Printed in China
SCP 10 9 8 7 6 5 4 3 2 1
4500379907

Photo Credits

Pages: 9 (left): Dr. Brian Matsumoto ◆ 9 (middle): Guy Cali/Corbis ◆ 10: Chris Rothfuss ◆ 11 (inset, shawl): Godley & Peers ◆ 19: Cody Sue Jones ◆ 24 (top right): Corbis ◆ 24 (bottom right): U.S. Army ◆ 25: U.S. Department of Defense ◆ 36 (left): Getty Images ◆ 42, 43: Lewis family ◆ 44: Eli Lilly and Company Archives ◆ 54, 58: Dr. Cecil Forsberg, University of Guelph, Ontario, Canada ◆ 55: Nick Suydam/Allamy ◆ 56 (left): SFL Botanical/Allamy ◆ 56 (right): GTC Biotherapies ◆ 57 (left): University of Kentucky ◆ 57 (right): www.glowfish.com ◆ 59 (left): Fotosearch ◆ 74 (left): NASA/Tony Gray and Tom Farrow

Contents

Dr. Randy Lewis holds a *Nephila clavipes,* a type of golden orb weaver spider.

SPIDER SILK: STRONGER THAN STEEL

DANGER LURKS. In a classroom near Dr. Randy Lewis's lab, five-year-old Zane sits perfectly still. Only his eyes shift…to the spider crawling on his face. It's a golden orb weaver, one of the largest web-spinning spiders on the planet. Now the spider sort of shakes its booty, attaching its silk to Zane. That way, if it falls, it won't shatter. You see, someone here is in danger, but it's not Zane; it's the spider. Spiders, though fierce insect hunters, are quite fragile themselves. If they fall, they can die. Luckily, the spider has a lifeline: its silk.

This silk — strong enough to bear the weight of the spider — is what compelled Randy and his team at the University of Wyoming to study the golden orb weaver. Zane's mother, Heather Rothfuss, is a scientist in Randy's lab and a member of this team. Zane and other scientists' children are frequent visitors.

Spider silk can be stronger than steel and even stronger than Kevlar, the material used in bulletproof vests. In the Spider-

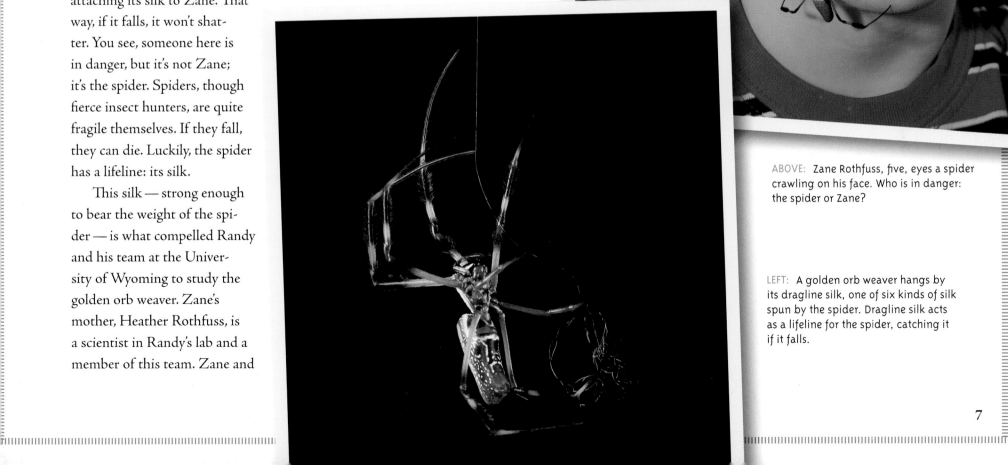

ABOVE: Zane Rothfuss, five, eyes a spider crawling on his face. Who is in danger: the spider or Zane?

LEFT: A golden orb weaver hangs by its dragline silk, one of six kinds of silk spun by the spider. Dragline silk acts as a lifeline for the spider, catching it if it falls.

Man movies, Peter Parker was able to swing from buildings, catch a falling car, and stop a speeding train — all with spider silk. Randy says that the strength of spider silk is not exaggerated in the movies. If anything, spider silk is even stronger. In real life, Peter Parker could stop a 747 airplane with a rope of spider silk just one inch in diameter.

Then again, in real life, a boy would not be able to shoot spider silk. Unlike in the movie, if Zane were bitten by the spider crawling on his head, he wouldn't turn into Spider-Man. Getting a nonspider to produce spider silk is more complicated than that. Zane isn't genetically designed to spin vast amounts of spider silk. To do so, he'd have to consume huge amounts of protein—say, eighty pounds of beef a day. Also, in order for him to shoot webs from his wrist, a silk gland would need to be in his arm. Zane could probably grow hair that was partial spider silk, but nobody is suggesting that this should or ever *would* happen. Outlandish possibilities such as humans making spider silk, while interesting, are just that: outlandish.

Zane is obviously genetically different from the spider. But what do we mean by "genetically"? It means that Zane's genome is different from the spider's genome. A genome is an organism's instruction manual. It tells the

The strength of spider silk wasn't exaggerated in the movie *Spider-Man.* A rope of spider silk just one inch thick could stop a 747 airplane—a real one, not just a toy.

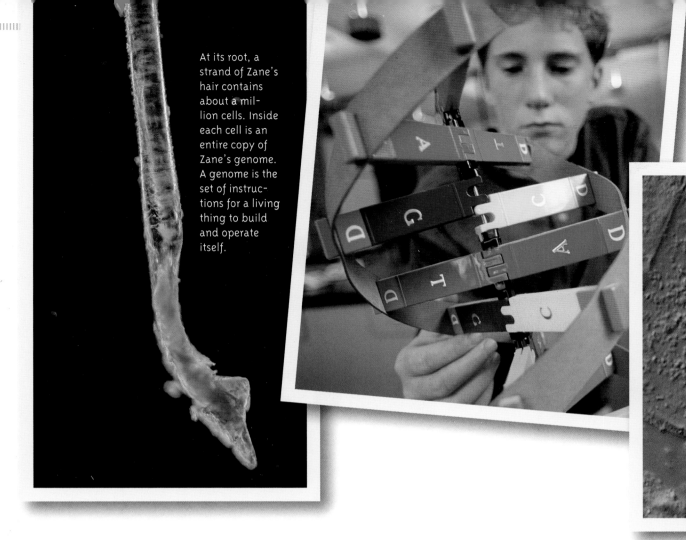

At its root, a strand of Zane's hair contains about a million cells. Inside each cell is an entire copy of Zane's genome. A genome is the set of instructions for a living thing to build and operate itself.

LEFT: DNA, deoxyribonucleic acid, is shaped like a twisty ladder. Each rung contains two chemical compounds, either adenine (A) and thymine (T) or guanine (G) and cytosine (C).

Your body contains millions of cells like this one. Within each cell is a nucleus (the circle at the center of this cell.) Each nucleus contains a copy of your genome. The genome is made of DNA.

organism how to build and operate itself. Each living thing has a genome. Where is Zane's genome? It is in each of the millions of cells in his body. Let's look closely at a strand of Zane's hair, on which the spider is crawling at this very moment. The root (the part that attaches to his head) contains about a million cells. Each cell has an entire copy of Zane's genome. The genome is made up of a chemical called deoxyribonucleic acid, or DNA. DNA is shaped like a twisty ladder. On each rung are two chemi-

cal compounds: either adenine and thymine or guanine and cytosine. They are nicknamed A, T, G, and C; and A always pairs with T, and G always pairs with C.

If you read the letters going up the ladder, they make three-letter words. Each word is an instruction for building an amino acid. Amino acids work together to build proteins. Let's look at the bigger picture: Several genetic three-letter words make up a genetic sentence, or a gene, and one or more genes give instructions

for making a protein. Proteins are key chemical compounds that are basic parts of plants and animals and help them function. Because we eat plants and often animals, proteins are in the food we eat.

Cells are tiny pieces that are the basis of all living things. There are different types of cells, but all contain DNA, which gives instructions for building proteins. Here's how: In the nucleus (the center of the cell) a section of DNA (the gene) is copied. That copy is called messenger ribonucleic acid (or mRNA). RNA is similar to DNA but made of slightly different chemicals. The mRNA (the copy of the gene) gives instructions for building a protein. It travels to the cytoplasm, which is the outer area of the cell. In the cytoplasm, ribosomes (which are made of proteins and RNA) read the mRNA. Following these directions, the ribosomes build the protein. As you can see, proteins (within the ribosomes) help build other proteins.

Zane's DNA tells his body to make many different proteins. One kind of protein is keratin, which makes up his hair. If Zane were Spider-Man, his DNA would give instructions for producing spider silk proteins. We can all agree that would be awesome. But Zane has different genes and, therefore, different proteins from those of a spider. Human genes are pretty awesome, too. They allow us to solve problems creatively. They allow scientists to make spider silk in new ways.

Zane's hair is blond and fine, like his mom's. His brother, Connor, seven, also has fine blond hair. Although all humans have the same genes, the genes have variations. These variations, called alleles, run in families. They cause family members to look alike. Animals

also share alleles with their family members. But all humans are quite similar, genetically, to one another. We all share 99.9 percent of our genomes. In fact, genetically, *all* living things are fairly similar. Even a human and a banana share 50 percent of their genes. That's because many genes are basic to life. They control cell activity, or work. Cells work together. They communicate, create food for other cells, and create new cells. Through this work, cells build plants and animals.

Let's look closely at the spider that has been crawling on Zane's face. Like Zane, it has genes. Like Zane, each hair — or seta, as it's called on a spider (plural, *setae*) — contains cells at the root. The cells contain copies of the spider's genome. The spider shares many genes with Zane. But unlike Zane, it has silk-spinning genes. Actually, this one spider can spin six types of spider silk, with varying strength and elongation (the ability to stretch without breaking). You see, in addition to being stronger than Kevlar, spider silk is stretchier than nylon.

Together, strength and elongation determine toughness (which is an actual measurement, not just an expression).

Imagine the possible uses for material this tough: Bulletproof vests. Parachute rope. The wire that helps stop huge fighter planes as they land on an aircraft carrier. On a smaller scale, spider silk thread could suture, or stitch, extremely delicate areas, such as the brain, eyeball, or spinal cord. Artificial ligaments and tendons could also be made from spider silk. These could repair ankle, knee, and shoulder injuries.

Heather Rothfuss, a scientist in Dr. Lewis's lab and Zane's mom, visits goats at the University of Wyoming with Zane's brother, seven-year-old Connor. Like many relatives, Heather, Zane, and Connor share traits. One example is their fine blond hair. Traits run in families because versions of genes called alleles run in families.

This shawl, made entirely of spider silk, was on display at the American Museum of Natural History. It took seventy people four years to collect enough golden orb weavers to spin all that silk.

Like a human hair, a spider's seta (which looks like a small black hair) also contains many cells at the root. Each contains a copy of the spider's genome.

Because of its toughness, people have sought spider silk for a long time. Ancient Greeks used it to dress wounds, for instance. But it has always been difficult to come by. Finding it in the wild is time consuming. Case in point: A golden shawl — eleven by four feet — went on display at the American Museum of Natural History. It took seventy people four years to collect enough golden orb weavers for the project, and another twelve workers to reel in the silk from the spiders.

11

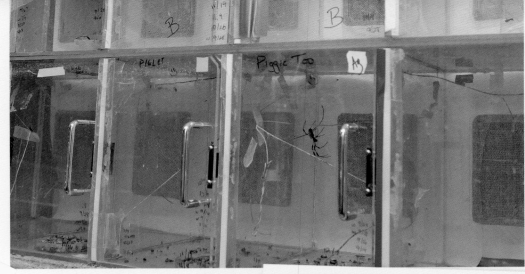

It would [...] ther webs if spiders could [...] is is how silk is produ[...] [...]rs, feedin[...] coco[...] can't th[...] out, let's visit th[...]

Randy and his team [...] weavers on hand. They reside [...] in the lab, each in a separate cage. The sp[...] crawling on Zane is named Spider from the Pink Cage. Some of her lab mates have more poetic names: Piggy (because she likes to eat), Piggy Two (who also likes to eat), and Ozzy (who attacks crickets as enthusiastically as the rock star Ozzy Osbourne once bit off a bat's head). Spider from the Pink Cage is named for, well, her pink cage.

While Spider from the Pink Cage rests, one of the scientists in the lab, Sherry Adrianos, holds Piggy Two. Sherry notes that, like humans, spiders are individuals. "They're so different from each other. Some are jumpy. Some come to you for the cricket. It sounds funny, but you get attached to them like a dog," Sherry says.

Though unique in some ways, all the spiders in Randy's lab have something in common: they're female. Only female golden orb weav-

are kept because they're the ones who spin ebs. The much smaller males don't. Instead, they steal insects from the female's web. Sometimes the female ignores the male. Other times, she attacks him. Yet the spider doesn't have to be male to become her lunch. She would gladly eat a female who entered her territory. As Sherry puts it, "If you try to raise spiders together, you'll be left with one big spider."

And now you know why spiders can't be raised domestically, like silkworms. They would eat each other. That's a shame, because spiders are great at producing spider silk. However, Randy thinks other organisms can be great at making spider silk, too. He has three candidates in mind: goats, silkworms, and alfalfa. In fact, the goats at the University of Wyoming are already producing spider silk protein.

Banana Spider

THE FEMALE GOLDEN ORB WEAVER is nicknamed the banana spider for her color and shape. But Sherry thinks of her as the ballerina spider because of her grace and "costume." Her step is so light, you can barely feel her crawling on your skin. She is gold and black, and tufts of fur decorate her long legs. She seems to be playing a role in *Rumpelstiltskin*, spinning golden silk. But rather than making the king rich, her golden web catches live meals for herself.

The golden orb weaver can spin a web—up to three feet wide—in less than an hour and make one hundred webs in a lifetime. (She lives approximately two years.) She tends to repair a damaged web rather than start over, as many other spiders do. However, when her web is destroyed, she may eat the silk, recycling the proteins from this nourishment to spin a new web.

The golden orb weaver is one of the largest spiders to spin a web. (There are larger spiders, such as tarantulas, but they live in nests or burrows.) Several species belong to the golden orb weaver family, including *Nephila komaci*. In that species, the female's body is 1.5 inches long, her legs, 4 to 5 inches. As with all golden orb weavers, the male is much smaller. The golden orb weavers in Randy's lab are *Nephila clavipes*.

You might come across a golden orb weaver—or its web—if you live in or visit warm places, such as Florida or Central America. Randy and his family encountered them in Central America during a family vacation.

A golden orb weaver can spin an intricate web such as this one in less than an hour and complete 100 in a lifetime.

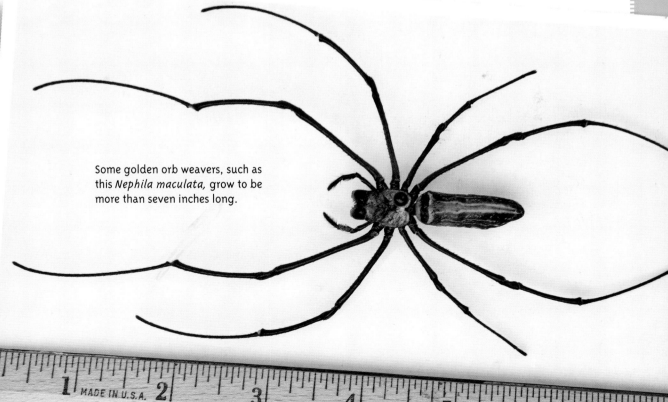

Some golden orb weavers, such as this *Nephila maculata,* grow to be more than seven inches long.

SPIDER GOAT, SPIDER GOAT

AT THE UNIVERSITY OF WYOMING Animal Sciences Livestock Center, Randy feeds Jackie. She looks very goatlike. She is, in fact, a goat. But she has a tiny bit of spider in her. She's a transgenic goat. A transgenic organism contains genes from another organism. The organism can be a plant, an animal, or simple-celled living thing, like a bacterium. Here's how a goat like Jackie becomes transgenic:

When they are embryos, the goats are injected with spider silk genes. When the goats grow up, they may pass these genes on to their baby goats (just as Heather passed the genes for blond hair to her boys). Now the babies are transgenic, too. Randy says that either Jackie's mother or father was implanted with the silk gene. Jackie and the other transgenic goats came from Nexia Biotechnologies, a Canadian company, now defunct. Randy supplied the spider silk genes, but he doesn't know the goats' full history. Many of the goats from Nexia have since had babies. The babies are at least second-generation transgenic goats. Not all the baby goats become transgenic. This is

because one parent is always transgenic and the other nontransgenic. Some baby goats inherit the nontransgenic parent's gene; others, the transgenic parent's gene.

Let's pause here. If spider goats sound like science fiction, you should know that they're possible because genes work the same way in

Randy milks Tiramisu. She is not part spider, so her milk doesn't contain spider silk proteins. The baby goats will drink this milk.

all living things. Goats and spiders both have genes. The genes are instructions for building proteins. In a transgenic animal, the transplanted gene isn't treated like a foreign gene. It's treated like any other gene—as instructions for building proteins. If the goat's genes say to produce spider silk proteins, then that's what the goat's body will do. Other than their special milk, the transgenic goats are like any other goats. All but one of their genes are goat genes. The goats were injected with only one spider gene, not the spider's entire genome.

Because Jackie is a transgenic female, her milk is special. It contains a small amount of spider silk protein. It will be taken back to the lab, where Heather will purify it until only the spider silk protein remains. At this point the protein is a powder. The powder will be placed in liquid chemicals and spun into spider silk.

Jessie is as cute and playful as a puppy. But she's almost all goat (and a little spider).

Jackie is producing milk because she recently gave birth to baby goats—twins! They're romping around like puppies in a pen a few feet away. Jackie's baby goats (called kids) are Jessie and an unnamed boy. They're playing with Aurora and her twin brother, also unnamed. Aurora and her brother belong to Tiramisu, a mother who's *not* transgenic but is a good milker. Their father, Chewy (so named because he sounds like Chewbacca from *Star Wars*), is transgenic. Uzi is the father of Jessie and her twin brother. He's not transgenic.

In addition to the goat kids, there are two human kids in the pen: Morgan, eight, and Andrew, ten. They sometimes help their dad, the scientist Justin Jones, take care of the goats. A big part of caring for animals is playing with them, and Andrew and Morgan are good at that! The goats nip at Andrew's shirt and prance around him. He picks them up and snuggles them.

While Andrew helps his dad with something else, Morgan tries to get the goats to drink milk from the bucket. The goats have recently been weaned, meaning they no longer drink milk from their mothers. They still drink goat's milk—Tiramisu's. Her milk doesn't contain the valuable spider silk proteins. If the goats drank Jackie's milk, they would not become transgenic. But it would be a waste of spider silk proteins.

The milk bucket looks like a collection of human baby bottles. Just as it's easy for a baby to drink from a bottle, it should be easy for the goat kids to drink from the bucket. But the kids are rebelling against Morgan. They don't want the milk in the bucket. It's too cold! They want their mother's warm milk.

Justin says the milk has to be cold so that the baby goats don't drink too much and become "bum" goats—goats with potbellies.

ABOVE: They rebelled at first, but the kids decide to drink the cold milk after all.

LEFT: Sometimes the kids get rolly ankles. Then their ankles must be taped so that they don't bend too far. Jessie is a Packers fan just like one of the scientists.

That's not healthy for them. With cold milk, however, the goats might not drink enough. Justin has to make sure they do. Luckily, their instincts tell them to drink milk when they're hungry. They drink at least sixteen ounces (half a liter) a day. This is equivalent to two full-size human baby bottles. Goats typically can produce more than enough milk for their babies: four to six liters per day. But the first generation of transgenic goats tends to produce a little less. Jackie produces about one liter of transgenic milk a day. However, it's high in spider silk protein: three grams per liter.

The girl goats were named by Andrew and Morgan after classmates. (If you have classmates whose names you like, perhaps you'll name goats after them someday!) The scientists in Randy's lab think the goats are really cute. (Heather describes them as a cross between puppies and deer.) The scientists especially dote on little Jessie, born at just one pound. The average goat weighs four pounds at birth. Her brother weighed five pounds. He must have gotten most of the nourishment in the womb. Scientists warmed the newborn Jessie under a heat lamp. They fed her plenty of milk. Jessie gained weight and grew stronger. Now she's as rambunctious as her siblings (but still smaller).

Jessie and her brother have a condition the scientists call "rolly ankles." It means their ankles bend too much. It's caused by overcalcification of the tendons. With medicine, it will heal. To keep the kids' ankles from twisting, another scientist, Holly Steinkraus, has taped them. The goats were born after the Green Bay Packers won a playoff game, and Holly, a football fan, loves the Packers, hence the green and gold.

The scientist Holly Steinkraus tests the goats' blood to see if they inherited the spider gene.

As cute as the goats are, the burning question in the scientists' minds is whether the baby goats will be transgenic. The more female transgenic goats there are, the more spider silk proteins can be produced through their milk.

On Monday, blood was drawn from the baby goats. Holly runs a test to see which goats are transgenic. She'll know the results on Wednesday. It's likely that only two of the four goats will be transgenic. This means that with only two female baby goats, the odds are that only one of the four babies will grow up to produce spider silk milk.

Those aren't great odds. Also, Randy says that it's not enough for the transgenic goats to produce spider silk proteins. They have to produce a large quantity. That requires them to be good milkers and for their milk to be rich in spider silk protein. Jackie's milk is high in silk protein, but she doesn't produce much milk.

To see what Randy is doing in hopes that future generations will milk better, we leave this barn, which houses only Tiramisu, Jackie, and the babies. We are off to visit the male goats—the billies.

18

Born on the Fourth of July

FREEDOM WAS A TRANSGENIC GOAT born prematurely on the Fourth of July. She couldn't stand or nurse. Her mother didn't take good care of her. (This isn't uncommon among first-time animal mothers.) Justin brought Freedom home. Justin and his wife, Cody, had experience with preemies. Their son Morgan was born prematurely. Cody is also a pediatric nurse.

Justin fed Freedom through a tube. Cody kept Freedom warm. Human preemies are kept warm in an incubator. To keep Freedom warm through the cold Wyoming nights, Cody wrapped her in plastic wrap and kept her by the fireplace. During the day, Freedom sunbathed with Cody. Andrew and Morgan helped, too, by feeding Freedom bottles of milk.

After a couple of days Freedom could walk. She followed the family around like a puppy! She also palled around with their real-life puppy, Sable, a ten-pound fluffy Pomeranian. Together they looked like stuffed animals come to life.

Though on the go, Freedom still needed to stay warm. Cody's coworker knitted her a red, white, and blue sweater. The goat went with the family to a company picnic. Eventually she was strong enough to join the herd. But she never saw herself as a goat. She refused to follow the herd into the pens. She was a pampered pet, not a goat! Though she grew as strong as the other goats, she eventually died of pneumonia, a disease that plagues all goats—whether transgenic or not.

Freedom, a transgenic goat born prematurely, hangs out with her pal Sable, a Pomeranian.

SILK MILK

THE BILLY GOATS—seven in all—are kept separate from the females. The barnyard is wild. The males jump on one another's backs to show dominance. They butt heads when they eat. They also wear a rather *interesting* cologne. Goats are capable of urinating at 180 degrees. They soak the front of themselves — up to their beards — with urine as part of their mating ritual. If you're familiar with the stinky old billy goat stereotype, it's true. But another stereotype — that goats will eat anything — isn't. Justin says these goats are picky eaters. When given alfalfa, they'll set the stems aside and eat only the leaves.

These are typical billies, except, of course, that they are part spider. All but one is transgenic. Chewy, the father of Aurora and her twin brother, is transgenic. Uzi, the father of Jessie and her twin, is not. Randy selected Uzi to be their father in hopes that his babies would be better milk producers. Of course Uzi is not a good milk producer himself. As a male, he doesn't produce milk at all. But Uzi comes from a long line of good milkers. (He also comes from a farm that names its animals after countries; his nickname is short for Uzbekistan.)

Again, it comes down to genetics. Just as spiders pass on silk-making genes to their young and parents pass down hair type, goats

RIGHT: The fathers of the four kids are the two biggest goats: Chewy, right, who is transgenic, and Uzi, left, who is not.

pass on milking traits to their babies. Instead of doing genetic testing, Randy uses old-fashioned farm sense. To get good milk producers, he breeds a "spider goat" with a goat whose family members produce lots of milk.

Next we drive to the barn that houses the females, known as does or nannies. There are more nannies than there were billies — thirty in all — but it's calmer here. We join them inside the fence, which we didn't do with the rambunctious billies.

The does like visitors, and a few jump up on us. Federal regulations say that animals in scientific studies must have enrichment. There must be more to their lives than testing. At Nexia, the goats had a play mountain and a goat entertainer who played ball with them. Here they have student and children visitors instead. A goat nips at my notebook and tries

ABOVE: Even though there are many more does than billies, the doe pen is calmer than the billy barnyard.

LEFT: Pudge gives Justin a friendly hello as Freckles strikes a pose. Named for her Freckly nose, she is the best milker in the herd and may also be the only one who poses to have her picture taken.

Tank acts
as a companion to
does who are giving birth. Goats
don't like to be alone, but for their safety, birth
shouldn't take place around others in the herd.

to pull it away. When students visit the herd, the goats sometimes give them a hard time. One tore a paper out of a graduate student's hand and led her on a wild-goose chase. Luckily, the goats let me keep my notebook!

One of the best milkers in the herd is Freckles (named for the spots on her nose). Randy says that even when she's not pregnant, her milk vein is visible. The milk vein delivers blood to the milk ducts. That leads to better milking. Right now, Freckles is pregnant. In the past, she has birthed a single kid, twins, and triplets. She is a first-generation spider goat. That is, she's the first generation to be bred at

the University of Wyoming. Because she came from Nexia, her complete family history is unknown. Randy's team has found that their first-generation transgenic goats don't produce much milk. With the second generation, the milk production goes up. The hope is that the third generation (which will be the babies of Freckles's, Jackie's, and Tiramisu's babies) will produce even more.

Freckles and Tank are the alpha does. Tank, so named for the way she head-butts the other does for a turn at the trough, had a C-section during her first birth and can no longer reproduce. She is kept as a companion animal. When

another nanny goes into labor, Tank is placed in the pen next door. Goats are social and don't like to be alone, but at the same time, they must give birth in isolation. Otherwise, another female might think the babies are hers. The real mother would fight her, and a female or baby goat might get hurt.

On average, each goat gives birth to two kids.

Not every goat that the scientists try to breed ends up giving birth. Jackie and Tiramisu were only two of nine nannies that the scientists had hoped to breed in the first round. That's a lower rate than usual; Randy says they may have been bred a little too early in the season.

For now, Jackie's milk is the only milk being collected. Justin picks it up at the barn and brings it to Heather at the lab. Heather must purify the milk so that only spider silk proteins remain. She has her work cut out for her! The process begins in a chilly little room inside the lab. The room is 39 degrees Fahrenheit (4°C.) Within the room is a cooler, which is -4 degrees F (-20°C.) The room and cooler are similar in temperature to your refrigerator and freezer at home.

Inside the freezer are four hundred gallons of milk. All of it contains spider silk protein. You wouldn't want to drink this milk — but not because of the spider silk proteins. That alone wouldn't hurt you (and it wouldn't turn you into Spider-Man). You wouldn't want to drink the milk because some of it is five years old and curdled! Also, it's not sanitary. Dairies — whether cow, goat, or sheep — follow certain sanitary steps while milking, and then they pasteurize the milk. This kills bacteria, such as harmful *E. coli.* Neither precaution has been taken with this milk because it's not for drinking.

Outside the freezer is the tangential flow

The goats produce milk faster than it can be purified. The freezer is full of spider milk.

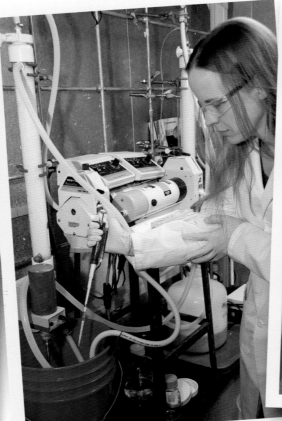

Heather sends the spider milk through the tangential flow filtration (TFF) machine, the first step in purification.

The large proteins and fat are left in this bucket. In a dairy operation, this would be used to make cheese.

filtration (TFF) machine — the first step in purification. There's a bucket on the left side of the TFF and one on the right. The bucket on the left contains raw white milk. A tube filters out the casein proteins and fat, which make up 80 percent of the milk. That stuff is left in the bucket. The rest of the milk is pushed through another filter and into the bucket on the right. At this point it's a clear liquid called whey. The same process is used in cheese making. The cheese curds would be in the left bucket and the whey in the right. In the popular nursery rhyme, Little Miss Muffet eats both: "Little Miss Muffet sat on a tuffet, eating her curds and whey. Along came a spider who sat down beside her and frightened Miss Muffet away." Her snack was actually cottage cheese. Miss Muffet would surely be horrified by spider goat cottage cheese!

Heather takes the whey to another lab room. She explains that she is going to "do chemistry" to the milk. She slowly adds ammonium sulfate (a salt) to the whey until the spider silk protein precipitates (falls out of the liquid). You can see the protein at the bottom of the beaker. Next, the protein is freeze-dried until only a powder remains. The protein is dissolved into liquid chemicals. This is called spindope. The spindope is spun into spider silk.

Voilà! Our question is answered. Of the three candidates (goats, silkworms, alfalfa), the goats should make spider silk. Because they already *are* making spider silk. Right? The end. Well . . . not quite. As you learned

Heather tests the whey for spider silk proteins.

BELOW: Heather adds ammonium sulfate to the whey.

earlier, the goats haven't made vast quantities of spider silk proteins. Not all products require large amounts. Sutures for surgery, for instance, would require very little. But to create something like parachute rope, Randy would need lots of silk. In that case, another spider silk protein–producing candidate might be better. Perhaps even a plant.

The last step of purification happens in a machine called the lypholizer. It freeze-dries the spider silk solution so that only the spider silk proteins remain.

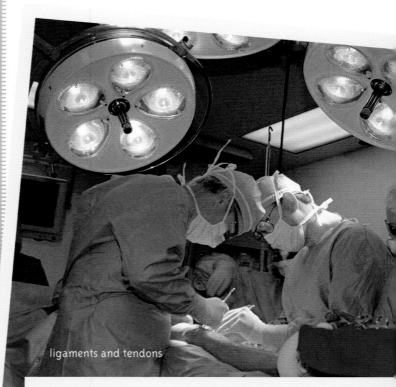

ligaments and tendons

bulletproof vests

Potential Spider Silk Products

Ligaments and tendons. Because of its strength and flexibility, spider silk could be used to make artificial ligaments or tendons. Currently, cadaver ligaments and tendons are used.

Surgical sutures. Because spider silk is so strong at a small diameter, these sutures could allow doctors to perform delicate procedures, such as eye, brain, or spinal cord surgery.

Fishing line. For the same reason, spider silk could be used as a thinner and thus less visible fishing line than what's currently on the market. It would also be stretchier. Fish could tug on the line without snapping it.

Parachute rope. Because of its flexibility, spider silk parachute rope would have some give. That way, skydivers wouldn't be jerked when their parachutes opened.

Airplane arresting wire. A fighter plane landing on an aircraft carrier has a relatively short runway. To stop it, a steel wire is strung across the runway. A hook on the aircraft catches the wire. The wire unwinds below deck, so that it moves with the plane, gradually slowing the aircraft down. As the plane approaches the end of the runway, the wire stops unwinding. Now the plane comes to a complete stop. Since spider silk is stronger than steel, it would make a stronger wire. It could also stretch as the plane slowed down, rather than unwinding belowdecks.

Space suits. Spider silk can retain its strength and flexibility under extreme cold. Because space is extremely cold, spider silk could be one of the fibers in space suits.

Bulletproof vests. Because spider silk is stronger than Kevlar, it has been proposed as a more lightweight material for bulletproof vests. Randy says that the silk would need to be less stretchy than current bio-engineered silk. Otherwise, the vest would stop the bullet but stretch to the point that both the vest and bullet went through the body.

ABOVE: airplane arresting wire

GROWING SILK? EXPERIMENTING WITH ALFALFA

RANDY AND HIS WIFE, Lorrie, grew up on farms in Wyoming — he in Garland, she in Ralston. They were sweethearts at Powell High School. Now they live on a sixty-acre farm overlooking the eastern Rocky Mountains. Their children, Brian and Karren, are grown. Brian is an orthopedic surgeon. He is married to Audey, and they have two sons. Karren is a science teacher with Teach for America. A third child, Daryl, passed away at age two from a heart condition.

Along the base of the mountains, coal trains roll by. Wyoming is the biggest coal producer in the country. In the summer, Lorrie, an accountant, has a vegetable garden with carrots, spinach, lettuce, and zucchini. Tomatoes won't grow here. The summer is too short and chilly.

During the summer the sheep graze in the pasture, but now it's winter. Snow blankets the frozen grass. The sheep eat from troughs in the barnyard. Wyoming has more sheep than people (about a million sheep and half a million people). Randy owns twenty-eight of those sheep. The females, or ewes, pace the barnyard skittishly. Though related to goats (both belong to the bovine subfamily Caprinae), the sheep behave differently. They're not as playful. They seem afraid. Randy says that they can recognize faces. They know his, but not that of Andy Comins (the photographer) or mine. They keep their distance until Randy pours corn feed into their troughs. Then they come running.

ABOVE: During winter in Wyoming, the ground is frozen and blanketed with snow. Sheep eat alfalfa in the barnyard.

BELOW: Though sheep and goats are closely related, the sheep aren't as friendly as the goats. They're skittish around visitors.

Randy and his wife, Lorrie, raise twenty-eight sheep on their ranch along the Eastern Rocky Mountains.

Randy cuts and bales hay for the sheep to eat in the winter.

Some of Randy's young neighbors are in 4-H, a youth program in which children raise and sell livestock. Randy's neighbors keep their sheep here, and they name them. Randy, who has raised sheep since he was a boy, calls them by their numbers. He does pause to chat. "What's up, old girl?" he says to one, patting her head.

The male sheep, like the goats, are separated from the females. Schaefer, Mac, and Wesson, the three males, are in a pen inside the barn. Other stalls in the barn are blanketed with soft grass, as fluffy as an Easter basket. Randy grew the grass on the farm, cut it with the tractor, and then baled it. For much of the year the ground is frozen, so it's important to have lots of hay on hand for feed. This particular hay has a special purpose. In a few days lambs will be born in the grassy stalls. Most will be twins.

RIGHT: Late in January, many sheep are close to giving birth. They eat alfalfa, which is high in protein, so that the lambs will be healthy.

155

Unlike with the goats, there's no reason to wean the babies quickly. The milk isn't used for science or sold as a dairy product. The lambs will rest in the stalls with their mothers for a while.

The sheep typically eat corn and hay. But now, while they're pregnant, and later, when they're nursing, they also eat alfalfa. And so here on Randy's farm we come face-to-face with another spider silk protein candidate. Not the sheep (though they could possibly produce it in their wool), but the alfalfa.

Alfalfa is a major crop in Wyoming. Because of the high elevation, it can't be grown in Laramie. But in northern Wyoming, where Lorrie's family still farms, it grows just fine. Being familiar with the crop, Randy looked to alfalfa for spider silk production. For one thing, it's high in protein. Proteins are good for the lambs, and are also key components of all living things. But cells, and thus the living things, also contain carbohydrates and fats. The plants that are higher in protein are good candidates for making spider silk, because it is a protein, too, so higher-protein plants would produce more spider silk protein. The high-protein content also makes alfalfa nutritious feed for animals. After the spider silk proteins are extracted, the alfalfa can be recycled as animal feed.

Of course Randy's sheep are eating regular alfalfa. To see the spider alfalfa, we travel back to Randy's lab. Holly Steinkraus leads the alfalfa project. First she cuts leaves off wild-type alfalfa. (Wild-type doesn't mean

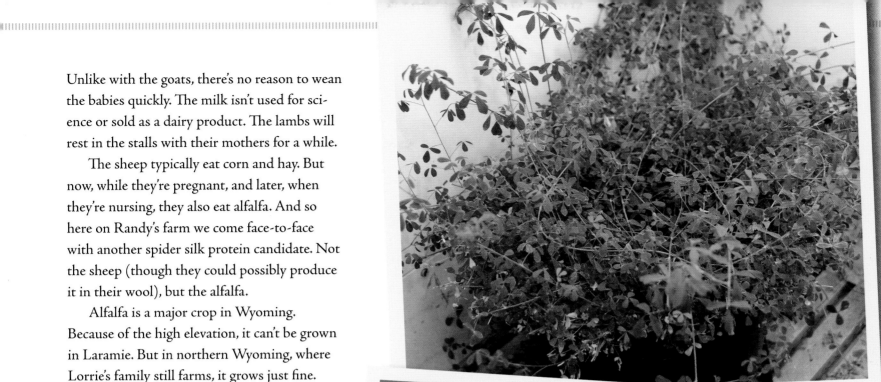

LEFT: Alfalfa, shown here growing in the lab, is a nutritious plant in the pea family. It provides many animals with the protein they need.

LEFT: Holly Steinkraus began work on the spider alfalfa project in 2002.

29

Leaves of wild-type
alfalfa are infected
with the spider gene.

The alfalfa, now containing the spider
silk gene, is allowed to grow as callus.

that it grows in the wild, but rather that it is nontransgenic. The wild-type alfalfa is still a domesticated plant.) Holly creates agrobacteria that contain the spider silk gene. Agrobacteria are bacteria that infect plants. She allows the agrobacteria to attack the plant. In this case, they infect the alfalfa with the spider silk gene. Then she moves the alfalfa to a special solution. This solution causes the leaf cells to divide and lose their identity. Now they are callus. On plants, callus is a mass of cells similar to an early animal embryo. Usually, a cell's genome tells the cell what kind of cell it is. For instance,

it could be a leaf cell or a root cell. But callus cells aren't any particular type of cell. Together, they don't look like any part of a plant. They look like something chewed up and spit out. The callus is put in a series of different solutions. Each solution allows different parts of the plant to grow, such as the root or the shoot. Eventually it grows to be a whole plant. Because it was created from the infected leaves, it is a spider plant.

The alfalfa program isn't as far along as the goat program. Work began in 2002. Right now Holly is trying to get the spider silk genes

into the plants. Then she's testing whether the plants also have the spider silk protein. The challenges of engineering spider alfalfa are many: First, it's hard to infect the leaves with the bacteria that carry the silk gene. Second, the alfalfa often tests positive for the spider gene but turns out not to make the spider silk protein. Finally, it takes ten months to cultivate the alfalfa from the leaf stage to the plant stage. It's difficult to keep the plants going for that long, particularly indoors. Eventually the transgenic alfalfa will be crossed with a field cultivar (a crop plant) to make it more hardy. Before

The young plants are transferred to a new solution to further their growth.

The spider alfalfa grows as sprouts.

that can happen, the alfalfa needs to be transgenic. Once the alfalfa is made to produce the spider silk protein, the protein will be purified and spun, just like the protein from the goats' milk.

There is a final candidate for making bioengineered spider silk. The beauty of this organism is that it's capable of spinning its own silk. It's been doing so for millions of years, and humans have woven the silk for thousands of years. It's the silkworm.

31

Fun Activity: Isolate DNA from Strawberries!

HAVE YOU EVER EATEN DNA? By now you must know the answer. Every living thing has DNA, so when you eat fruits, vegetables, or animals, you eat DNA. You can isolate DNA from a fruit in your own classroom. Strawberries are ideal for this experiment because they have eight copies of their genome in each cell.

Remember, the genome is a living thing's instructions for making itself. Most fruits and vegetables have only two copies in each cell. Humans only have two, also.

Before you start this experiment, look closely at a whole strawberry. The leaves and the fruit look very different. Would you believe that they contain the same DNA in each cell? All of the cells in any given organism contain the same DNA, or genome. DNA is the physical substance. It contains the genome, which is the set of instructions. Think of the DNA as the book and the genome as the story. The genome tells each cell which genes to turn on. In the leaf cells, for instance, the genes for leaf-building proteins are turned on.

Caution: Though food is used in this experiment, it is not safe to eat or drink the mixtures, as they contain poisonous chemicals.

For four students you'll need:
4 strawberries, leaves removed
4 sealable plastic bags
4 coffee filters
4 clear cups or jars
4 Popsicle sticks or plastic spoons
1 cup water
2 teaspoons salt
4 teaspoons clear, unscented hand dish-washing liquid
½ cup 90 percent isopropanol (rubbing alcohol)

Directions:
1. Place one strawberry in each plastic bag. Mash the strawberry, being careful not to break the bag.

What's happening? This separates the cells from one another for the next step.

2. Mix the salt, dish liquid, and water. Pour this mixture, in equal parts, into the bags.

3. Mix the contents of each bag (while still in the bags) for two minutes.

What's happening? The mixture is breaking open the cells. The DNA inside

Each student needs one strawberry.

Step 4

the cells is released into the liquid.

4. Place the coffee filter over the cup. Carefully pour the contents of the bag into the filter, allowing the liquid to drip into the cup. Gently squeeze the filter to get most of the liquid. Discard the filter with the strawberry pulp.

What's happening? There is DNA in the liquid. There is still DNA in the pulp, too, but it's trapped in unbroken cells.

Protein, cellulose, and pieces of straw-berry cells are also in the pulp.

5. Slowly add 1/8 cup of isopropanol to each cup. Do not mix or stir. Wait.

6. You will see the DNA rise to the top. It looks like a little blob of slime.

7. Pick it up with a spoon or Popsicle stick. Behold the secret of life: DNA!

Yes, it does kind of look like snot.

What's happening? Normally the DNA is dissolved in the fruit. That's why you can't see it. The DNA was also dissolved in the liquid in the cup. The isopropa-nol, along with the salt you added earlier, pushed the DNA out of the liquid. Now you can see the DNA.

Step 7

SPIDER SILK . . . FROM SILKWORMS?

UNLIKE SPIDERS, silkworms can easily be raised together. They don't eat each other. They don't even have to be caged. They're raised in open baskets filled with leaves. They don't crawl away, because everything they could ever want (which is mulberry leaves) is in that basket.

In fact, mulberry silkworms, or *Bombyx mori*, have been raised domestically for thousands of years. Sericulture, as it's called, began in China about seven thousand years ago. The practice spread throughout Asia and then to the Middle East and Europe. At the time, only natural fibers, such as silk, wool, hemp, and cotton, were available. Today, man-made fibers can be woven into clothing. But fine garments, such as wedding gowns and men's ties, are often still sewn from silk cloth.

It's easy to see why silkworms are being studied as possible spider silk producers. They spin a lot of silk. Contrary to their name, they're not worms, but moth caterpillars. Each moth lays hundreds of eggs. When they hatch, they're as tiny as eyelashes. After molting (shedding their skin) five times, they grow to about two and a half inches. Then they spin their cocoons. Within several hours, each will have spun a cocoon with a single thread more than a thousand yards (914 meters) long. Inside the cocoons they metamorphose into moths. After a couple weeks the moths emerge from the cocoons. The moths mate and lay new eggs. In silk production, the cocoons are heated to kill the moths before they can emerge. Allowing the moths to emerge would damage the silk.

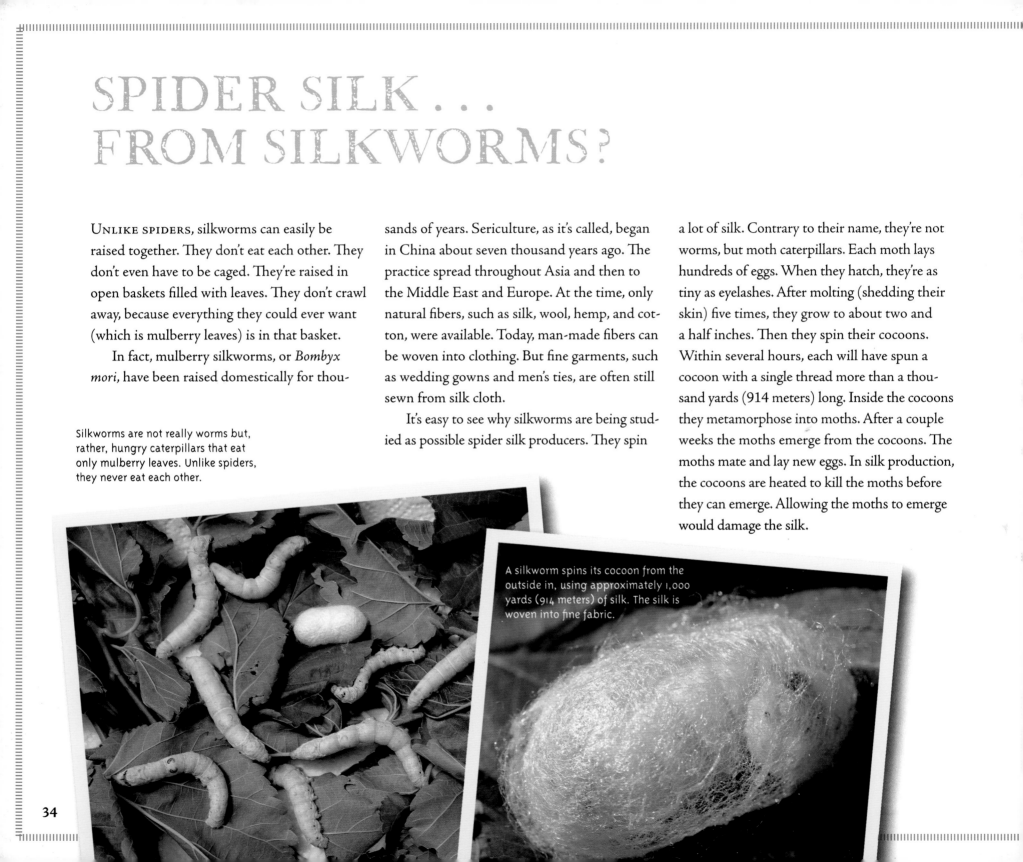

Silkworms are not really worms but, rather, hungry caterpillars that eat only mulberry leaves. Unlike spiders, they never eat each other.

A silkworm spins its cocoon from the outside in, using approximately 1,000 yards (914 meters) of silk. The silk is woven into fine fabric.

The eggs are pale at first. As the tiny larvae develop inside, the eggs will turn dark purple.

In commercial silkworm production, cocoons are heated to kill the silk-worms before they emerge from the cocoons, which would damage the silk.

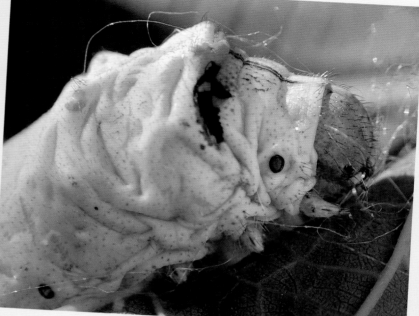

A silkworm has spinnerets, much like a spider. But the silkworm's spinnerets are in its mouth, whereas a spider's are in its posterior.

Like a spider, a silkworm makes silk in glands in its abdomen and spins it with spinnerets. A spider's many spinnerets are in its posterior, whereas the silkworm's two spinnerets are in its mouth. And while a spider spins many kinds of silk, silkworms spin identical fibers with both spinnerets. The fibers contain three proteins — heavy chain, light chain, and P25. Each fiber is coated in a gluelike substance called sericin. This causes the two fibers to stick together when spun. It also holds the

These are regular silkworm cocoons. Florence Teulé keeps them in the lab to compare their silk with that of the spider silkworms.

cocoon together. In silk production, boiling the cocoons washes away the sericin. Then the threads can be unwound. This means that if silkworms produced spider silk, the scientists wouldn't have to purify or spin it. The silk would already be spun!

Today the spider goats produce enough spider silk protein for medical applications. But if spider silk could be mass-produced, it could also be used for airplane arresting wire, car airbags, and maybe even clothing. Are silkworms the answer to mass-producing spider silk?

Florence Teulé, a scientist in Randy's lab, has been investigating this with collaborators Don Jarvis, a scientist at the University of Wyoming, and Malcolm Fraser, a scientist at the University of Notre Dame. Randy and Flo have some silkworms in the lab. They're in open plastic containers — eating mulberry leaves, of course. These silkworms are a naturally occurring white eye species. Flo explains that when she and the team engineered the spider silk gene, they linked it to a red eye gene. If the silkworms had red eyes, the team knew that the caterpillars had the spider silk gene. A fluorescent gene was also linked to the spider silk gene. It was hoped that silkworms with the spider silk gene would spin fluorescent silk. This would show that they not only had the spider silk gene but were also producing spider silk proteins. The silkworms currently in the lab don't have the spider silk gene. Flo needs these wild-type silkworms in order to compare their silk to transgenic silkworm silk. (Again, wild doesn't mean undomesticated. All mulberry silkworms are domesticated. Rather, it means nontransgenic. Likewise, nontransgenic goats are sometimes referred to as wild-type. They are domesticated goats, though.)

In the lab, silkworms eat powdered and cooked mulberry leaves. Mmm . . . they're still mulberry leaves and still delicious.

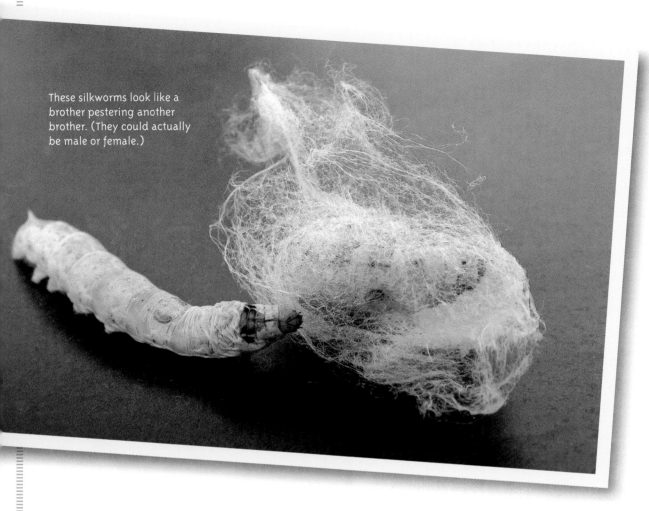

These silkworms look like a brother pestering another brother. (They could actually be male or female.)

Presently, the silkworms are spinning cocoons. Two silkworms are placed on the lab surface so that Andy can photograph them. (He thinks they look like Japanese bullet trains because of their streamlined heads and bodies.) One rolls gently inside its partially woven cocoon (which is spun from the outside in). The other silkworm hasn't begun spinning yet.

Randy says, "There's always a slacker." While Andy photographs them, the slacker silkworm crawls over another silkworm, which is spin-ning its cocoon. Flo jokes that he's annoying his brother. We don't know that they're males, but they do look like brothers wrestling. Flo says that the "slacker brother" is actually search-ing for a tight spot to spin his cocoon. In the container, another silkworm has attached to a piece of paper, which naturally folds over. This is how silkworms might have attached to mul-berry leaves on a tree. The slacker silkworm will probably attach to his brother's cocoon. The cocoons will be stuck together. That won't hurt

them. Inside the cocoons the silkworms will separately form pupae and metamorphose into moths. These silkworms are spinning regular silk. But recently silkworms were made to spin spider silk in their cocoons.

The Lewis, Jarvis, and Fraser labs collabo-rated to create transgenic silkworms. First, Flo and Don engineered the spider silk genes that would be injected into the silkworms. They sent the genes to scientists at Notre Dame.

At Notre Dame, silkworm moths were allowed to mate. Scientists harvested their eggs and placed them on slides. Next, scientists injected the spider silk DNA into the larval eggs. They were targeting the gonads. Gonads are reproductive organs. Cells located in the gonads are sex cells. Genes within sex cells are passed on to the next generation. Other genes are not. By targeting the sex cells, scientists ensured that future generations would be trans-genic, as opposed to only those silkworms that were injected. Scientists plugged the holes from the injections with superglue. Several thousand eggs were injected. Of those that became trans-genic, the scientists selected a male and female.

Now they had an "Adam and Eve." Adam and Eve mated. Eve laid hundreds of eggs, many of which grew to be transgenic silk-worms. The transgenic silkworms spun cocoons. The Notre Dame scientists sent the cocoons to Flo and Don at the University of Wyoming. They tested the silk from these cocoons to see if they contained spider silk. It was also important that the spider silk be in the silk fiber instead of the sericin, or coating glue. Remember, that stuff is washed away during silk processing. If the spider silk was in the glue, it would be washed away, too.

The cocoons tested positive for spider silk! Next, to determine whether it was in the glue or the threads, Flo washed the cocoons with water and soap. Neither washed the spider silk away. Only a powerful chemical solution could separate the spider silk proteins from the silk. This meant that the spider silk was in the thread, not the glue. The thread was a mixture of spider silk and regular silk. Because it contained spider silk, the silk was tougher and stretchier than regular silk. That was a successful outcome.

But could silkworms be made to spin pure spider silk? That remains to be seen. The answer may determine who becomes the star spider silk producer. Will it be goats? Silkworms? Alfalfa? Or perhaps all three?

The silkworm work will continue to be a team effort by the Lewis and Fraser labs. Meanwhile the Lewis lab — Randy and his team — are moving to Utah State University. There, Randy has been given an offer of increased funding. He'll buy better equipment and run new tests in hopes of pushing spider silk out of the testing phase and into production. We'll join him there. But for now, we have more to learn in Wyoming. Namely, how did all of this come about?

The silkworms attach their cocoons to a surface, such as the side of a Tupperware container or a piece of paper.

The cocoon on the right is partially spider silk. The spider gene was linked to a fluorescent gene. If the silk is fluorescent, it indicates that the spider silk protein is present.

Silkworms: No Longer Wild and Free

HUMANS HAVE RAISED mulberry silkworms for so long that they are now completely domesticated. None exist in the wild. Their likely ancestor, *Theophila mandarina*, is still a wild moth. Many other wild silkworms exist, but they spin poorer quality silk. As for the mulberry silkworm, it can't survive in the wild. Silkworm moths don't fear predators. Escaping would be difficult anyway, as they've lost the ability to fly. You can easily hold a silkworm moth, just as you could a pet rabbit.

Some silkworms are allowed to mature and breed. Others are killed while still inside the cocoon. Otherwise the silk would be damaged as the moths emerged from their cocoons. Besides silk production, silkworms serve another purpose: snack food. Silkworm pupae are a popular Korean dish, called *beondegi*.

Traditionally, sericulture has been a home-based business. People raised silkworms in small buildings on their property or even in their attics. Today you can order them online and raise them at home or in the classroom.

One silkworm relaxes; another spins its cocoon; and a third metamorphoses inside a fully spun cocoon.

Silkworm pupae are also sold as a Korean dish, *beondegi*. Pupae are silkworms in the stage of metamorphosing inside the cocoons.

THE HUNT FOR SPIDER SILK GENES

Randy, the oldest of four siblings, grew up in Wyoming. His father, Jack, was in the military, so the family moved around. When Randy turned five, the family settled down across the road from Jack's parents' farm. Jack became a district attorney and a private practice lawyer. He didn't farm, but he liked to spend time outdoors with the family. He especially loved fly-fishing. Randy would often tag along with his dad and granddad, Ezra. Randy rode horses by the age of five and hunted pheasants by the time he was ten. He and his siblings, Cindy, Becky, and Tim, hunted, fished, camped, and helped their granddad on his farm. Randy remembers spending most of their time outside. "There weren't video games back then," he says.

When Randy was ten years old, a tragedy occurred. His father was killed in a car crash. He'd been planning a bid for the Wyoming governorship in 1962. Had he lived, he probably would have won. Randy's mother, Evelyn, had been a nurse before her children were born. After the accident she sought an education degree and became a teacher.

At around the same time, Randy's granddad developed emphysema, a disease of the lungs. Randy and his siblings picked up the slack on the farm. Ezra had raised cattle, but now he switched to a smaller animal: sheep. Because of his granddad's poor health, Randy soon took over the operation. That included driving a pickup truck at age twelve to buy feed and supplies, bottle-feeding lambs inside their home, and breeding the sheep. It didn't matter that Randy was just a young boy. "If you're on a farm and something needs to get done, you've got to do it or it won't get done," he says.

Randy also spent time studying and playing sports. In grade school he played football at recess. He and his classmates got to be pretty tough, as the playground was asphalt and they played tackle. In high school he played football and baseball, and he wrestled. A good student, he received a National Merit Scholarship his senior year and enrolled at the California Institute of Technology (Caltech).

After a childhood on the farm, the pursuit of an animal-related major wouldn't have been

A very young Randy watches his father clean a freshly caught fish while his uncle, Ed Collins, looks on.

Randy (farthest to the right) examines the ribbons his family's flock has won.

LEFT: Randy (back, standing), his father, Jack; his mother, Evelyn; and his siblings, Cindy, Becky, and Tim, pose for a family photo in their home. Randy was about ten years old. He and his siblings would soon take on more responsibility at home and on the farm.

surprising. Yet when it came time to choose a major, Randy selected math. He soon discovered that it wasn't for him. It seemed too removed from real life. He thought about what else he'd enjoyed in high school. "I had a high school chemistry teacher who let us do all kinds of fun stuff in the lab," he remembers. "That's where I went, and I was good at it." He studied chemistry, biochemistry, and protein chemistry. Little did Randy know that chemistry would lead him back to work with animals.

While Randy was in school, groundbreaking work occurred in the field of transgenics. In the early 1970s scientists created the first transgenic bacteria. In 1982 the FDA approved human insulin—produced by transgenic bacteria—as medication for diabetics. It was an important breakthrough. In the early 1900s,

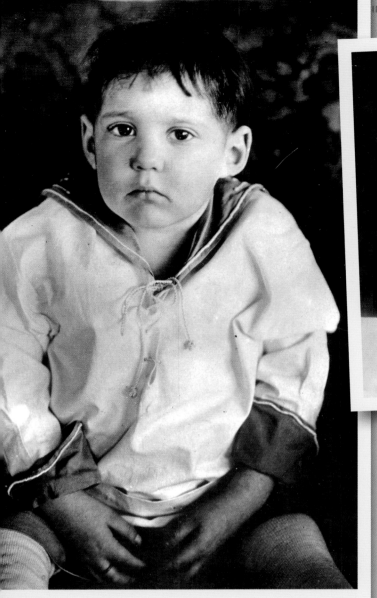

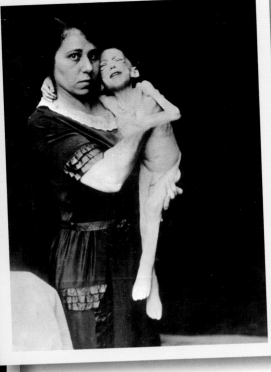

ming. He also consulted for a biotechnology company. The company asked whether silkworm silk could be produced through bacteria. Randy realized that bacteria could never outperform silkworms in silk protein production, but his research made him wonder if bacteria could produce *spider* silk. This question would shape the rest of his career.

The biotech company didn't pursue the study. As Randy finished his work for the company, he sought his own funding. His idea to produce spider silk through bacteria got two reviews: One said it was the greatest idea ever. The other said it was the stupidest idea ever. Luckily, the Office of Naval Research agreed with the first opinion. In 1988 they funded Randy's research, and he and his team set out to isolate spider silk proteins.

To study the mechanical properties of the spider silk, they had to "silk" the spiders. That means pulling the silk from the spinnerets. Scientists in Randy's lab still silk the spiders in order to send samples to researchers. Today Sherry Adrianos is silking Piggy Two. Sherry believes that all living things — even bacteria — have feelings. She is as kind as possible. At the same time, she believes that animal research is necessary. She says that anyone who has undergone surgery has reaped the benefits of animal research. "Where would we be as far as surgery? It's animal research that made it possible," she says.

She uses CO_2 (carbon dioxide) to relax the spider. Then she tapes Piggy Two onto a slide.

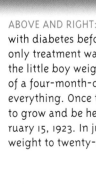

ABOVE AND RIGHT: J.L. was a three-year-old boy diagnosed with diabetes before insulin was available. At the time, the only treatment was a starvation diet. On December 15, 1922, the little boy weighed just fifteen pounds, the average weight of a four-month-old baby. The discovery of insulin changed everything. Once treated, patients could eat enough calories to grow and be healthy. The second photo was taken on February 15, 1923. In just two months, J.L. had nearly doubled his weight to twenty-nine pounds, a normal size for his age.

treatment for diabetes was basically starvation. Patients, including children, were limited to as few as four hundred calories per day. Through medical research Frederick Banting discovered that diabetics needed insulin. He first derived insulin from animal pancreases. With insulin, patients still followed a special diet but no longer had to starve. Transgenic bacteria provided a more efficient way to produce insulin. At around the same time, researchers created the first transgenic animals: fruit flies and mice.

These early breakthroughs in genetics laid the groundwork for Randy's career. After college, he and Lorrie married. In the early 1980s he went to work for the University of Wyo-

Piggy Two is taped down so that silk can be extracted. It will make her tired but will not hurt her. She is given a sip of water and a cricket before the process begins.

The scientist Sherry Adrianos pulls dragline silk out of Piggy Two.

Golden silk spools around a test tube.

She gives Piggy Two a sip of water — and a cricket as a treat. Now, with the slide under a microscope, she pulls at the silk with tweezers. This is dragline silk, the same kind that Spider from the Pink Cage spun as a lifeline in case she fell off Zane. Spiders also construct the frame and spokes of their webs with dragline silk. It's the strongest type of spider silk. In addition to holding the weight of a spider, it absorbs some of the shock when an insect crashes into a web.

Sherry connects the silk to a spool (a test tube). A machine rotates the spool. Piggy Two spins what could amount to a hundred yards (91 meters) of silk — the length of a football field. It shines like spun gold. In contrast, the artificial spider silk is white or opaque. Randy says that appears to be because of the spiders' diet. Since the reason is not central to their research, the team doesn't study it.

Early in Randy's research, scientists silked spiders in order to test the toughness of the silk. To determine the genes responsible for silk production, the team dissected the spider. Within the spider they found the seven glands that make the six types of spider silk and a gluelike substance. They took a DNA sample from each gland. Then they isolated the spider silk genes. This took a long time. Spider silk genes repeat over and over again. Remember the DNA letters we discussed earlier — A, T, G, and C — and how three letters combine to form a word? In spider silk, one word may repeat anywhere from 30 to 220 times. That made the genes hard to sequence. After two

years Randy had isolated the gene associated with MaSp1 (one of the proteins in dragline silk). (See the "Dragline Silk" sidebar.) This was big news in the scientific community. It was the first spider silk gene ever to be sequenced. A year later Randy and his team isolated the gene for MaSp2 (the other protein in dragline silk). They had cracked the genetic code for dragline silk. But it was only the beginning.

Dragline silk is one of six types of spider silk (see the "Different Types of Silk" sidebar). The scientists needed to study all types, because their physical properties — and possible uses — differ. A flexible spider silk like flagelliform would be ideal for ligaments, but

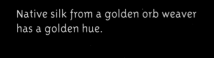

Native silk from a golden orb weaver has a golden hue.

BELOW: When Randy's team isolated a gene associated with dragline silk, it was front-page news in the scientific community.

not for bulletproof vests, for instance. Step by step, the team isolated all the genes, finishing in 2010 with piriform. Justin is studying its mechanical properties right now, so its potential uses are still unknown.

In the meantime, Randy moved forward with the information he had. Dragline silk was the strongest, and probably most desirable, silk. The team had already sequenced its genes. It was time to clone the genes and insert them into an organism. When making a transgenic organism, bacteria are a good starting point. Unlike goats, they reproduce quickly, require minimal care, and take up little space. There was just one problem. The genes, being so repetitive, were too big for bacteria. So the team designed "mini" versions of the spider silk genes. They inserted the mini genes into the bacteria. To see how this was done, we need only peer into Randy's lab.

Different Types of Silk

ORB WEAVERS PRODUCE six types of silk, plus a glue, each in a separate gland. Each silk has a different job. Some are found in the web. Others protect the spiders' eggs or are used to swathe prey.

* Major ampullate (dragline) silk: Composed of two proteins, dragline silk catches a spider when it falls and makes the outer frame and spokes of the spiderweb.

* Minor ampullate silk: This reinforces the web and provides scaffolding during its construction.

* Aciniform silk: Spiders wrap their prey in this swathing silk. It also forms the inner layer of the egg sac.

* Cylindrical gland silk: This forms the outer egg sac.

* Piriform silk: Spiders use this to attach a thread to an object or another thread.

Aciniform silk

- Flagelliform silk: Extremely flexible, this makes up the inner spirals of the web. It stretches as prey fly into the web, preventing them from bouncing off.

- Aggregate silk: This gluelike substance covers the flagelliform, further trapping prey.

Cylindrical gland silk

Dragline Silk

THERE ARE TWO PROTEINS in dragline silk: MaSp1 and MaSp2. The first gives the dragline silk its strength; the second, its stretchiness. In nature, the two are molecularly bound together. However, the goats produce either MaSp2 or MaSp1 in their milk—not both. The MaSp1 goats produce an average of 18.5 grams of spider silk protein per 6 liters of milk. MaSp2 goats produce much less—5 grams per 6 liters. The scientists mix the two proteins to make a fiber that is both strong and stretchy. The ratio changes based on whether the fiber needs to be stronger or stretchier.

Major ampullate (dragline) silk

FROM BACTERIA TO GOATS

Much of the work in Randy's lab involves bacteria. Bacteria provide a fast way to test spider silk genes. The scientists build mini spider silk genes. They inject them into bacteria. They make the bacteria multiply. Then the bacteria produce spider silk proteins. Scientists isolate the spider silk proteins. They spin the silk. They test the silk for strength and elongation. The bacterial silk won't perform as well as spider silk because the proteins are miniature. But comparing one mini protein to another is like comparing apples to apples. Whichever mini protein performs better will also perform better when it is full size. Eventually Randy's team will insert the full-size genes into goats and other organisms. They'll produce the proteins to make the ideal spider silk.

In her lab area Sherry has beakers full of millions of bacteria. You can't see the single-cell organisms, of course. They're microscopic. But you can smell them. One smells like an ape house. Another smells like garlic clam sauce. Like all living things, bacteria "eat." Sherry supplies the bacteria with nutrients, which they absorb through their liquid environment in the beaker. Depending on which spider silk proteins they're making, they metabolize the nutrients differently. This process is stinky. (If you've ever come across food that has spoiled,

Sherry is experimenting with spider silk proteins. This protein formed a flexible, cartilage-like material.

you, too, have smelled stinky bacteria!) Sherry has purified the spider silk proteins from the bacteria in these beakers. She needs to test the bacteria to make sure no spider silk proteins remain.

To make the spider bacteria, Sherry first designs the spider silk mini gene. Next she inserts the gene into the bacteria (a type of *E. coli*). To get the bacteria to multiply, she warms them to 98.6 degrees Fahrenheit (37° Celsius), your average body temperature. *E. coli* have evolved to multiply inside the human body. That's why bad strains of *E.coli* can make you so sick. Sherry is using a different type of *E. coli* (see sidebar "*E. coli* in the Lab"). A shaking incubator and fermenter also help the bacteria to multiply. The liquid is now murky from the bacteria.

Next, Sherry treats the bacteria with an antibiotic. If your doctor prescribes antibiotics, it's to treat a bacterial infection, such as strep throat. Antibiotics kill bacteria. In this case, the antibiotic will kill all the bacteria except those

that contain the spider silk gene. The spider silk gene is accompanied by a gene that has been designed to resist the antibiotic.

The spider silk genes are still inside the bacteria cells. The cells are broken open to release the DNA. This is done with an alkaline lysis. (If you did the strawberry experiment, you did the same thing to the strawberry cells with the dish soap and salt mixture.) When the DNA is "set free," the liquid becomes a gloopy, snotlike

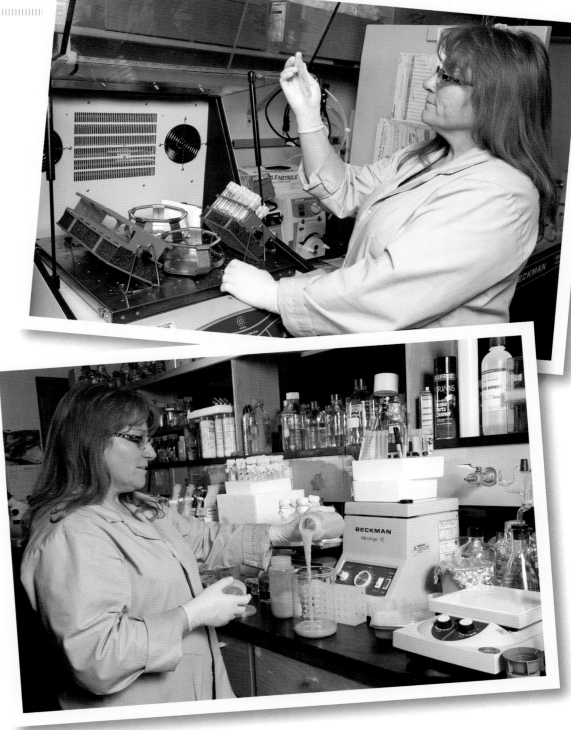

beige substance. It smells like cream of chicken soup. Finally, the DNA is isolated from this gloopy mixture.

The DNA is injected into new bacteria. This time the bacteria will make spider silk protein. Bacteria make other proteins, too. Through a simple process, all of these are removed until only spider silk protein remains. Randy's team is left with 2 to 500 milligrams of spider silk protein. The goat's milk provides much more — at least a gram. However, the bacterial process is faster. It allows the scientists to test many spider silk genes. Eventually they'll choose the best gene. They'll inject it into early goat embryos to create a new herd of spider goats.

By the late 1990s Randy's team had successfully bioengineered bacteria to produce spider silk. They were ready to move on to a bigger species. In 2000 Randy designed the first bioengineered spider silk genes for goats. Nexia, at its facility, injected an unknown number of goats. Only one, a male, became transgenic. He was the original spider goat. "That was perfect," Randy says. He explains that the male goat could mate with several females. When the females kidded, several transgenic babies were likely born. Randy never knew how many were born or how many generations were bred. He advised Nexia, but they kept much of the process secret. Then, in 2008, Nexia went out of business. Now Randy could bring the goats to Wyoming to study firsthand.

It was quite an adventure. For one thing,

TOP: Sherry has filtered the spider silk protein from the bacteria in these test tubes, but is testing the bacteria to make sure none remain.

ABOVE: The beige slime contains bacteria whose cell walls have been broken, setting the DNA free in the liquid.

51

the goats were quarantined because the U.S. Department of Agriculture considered them diseased and contagious. The spider genes weren't really contagious — no more than blue eyes or tallness is contagious — but the USDA had no other way of classifying transgenic animals. The quarantined goats traveled to Wyoming in a sealed trailer. Randy and Justin rushed them to their new home for food and water.

The current baby goats are descendants of the first spider goat. But are they transgenic? Holly is testing their blood now. First she breaks open the cell membrane. She isolates the DNA. This process takes about a day and a half. Next she amplifies certain sections. She doesn't make the DNA bigger, but rather she makes more copies. This is done by melting the DNA into two single strands. Now there are two halves of the gene. Each can be multiplied. Once the DNA is amplified, Holly can see the results on a gel. By Wednesday, the results are in.

In the meantime, the boy goats have been named. Holly named Jessie's twin Woody (for the *Toy Story* characters). Aurora's twin was named Borealis, or Boris for short. (Aurora borealis is the scientific name for the northern lights, streaks of light in the night sky that can be seen in latitudes toward the North Pole.)

The goats beat the odds. Both girls — Jessie and Aurora — are transgenic. Boris is also transgenic. Only Woody is wild-type. Back at the barn, the baby goats bounce around, as frisky as ever.

RIGHT: Holly tests the blood of Jackie's male kid, now named Woody.

They scratch their ears with their hind legs. They nip at Andy as he tries to take their picture.

Their enrichment activity is simple this afternoon. A bucket and its lid are flipped over for them to jump on. Aurora is the star of the bucket game. She jumps and dances on the lid. The other goats watch and learn. Little Jessie is next to try. She prances on the lid briefly. Aurora nudges her off. It's as if she doesn't want Jessie stealing her thunder!

The male kids are more timid at first. It's hard to believe they're young versions of rough-and-tumble billies. Boris eventually leaps onto the bucket. Like Aurora, Boris doesn't like Jessie the pip-squeak sharing "his" toy. He, too, head-butts poor Jessie off the bucket. Billies grow a full beard within a year. There are exceptions. One billy goat didn't grow his beard until he was two and a half or three years old. The scientists nicknamed him GQ — after the men's magazine — for his clean-shaven look. Once his beard came in, they renamed him

Frankie. "Now he was just a stinky old billy goat," Justin says.

While in the barn, the goats are pampered. Justin says that when the goats first came from Nexia, the scientists hoped not to get attached. That didn't work. Soon they were naming the goats and discussing their unique and often funny personalities. The sad truth is they can't keep all the goats. Nontransgenic males in particular are euthanized. This is because many fewer males than females are needed for breeding. Unfortunately, they can't be sold, as the FDA has not approved any transgenic animal for human consumption, including milk from those animals. The only goats that can be sold — either as pets or livestock — are nontransgenic babies of nontransgenic mothers, or nontransgenic mothers who have never had a transgenic baby. Tank is an example of a goat

BELOW: In toddler like fashion, Boris won't share the lid with Jessie.

that could be sold. Justin and Holly are working on a paper to prove that transgenic genes don't spread in the womb from mother to kid, kid to mother, or twin sibling to sibling. We'll find out later whether or not their paper may change this rule.

Randy's lab can't keep all the goats. The herd would become too large and unmanageable. Under those conditions, scientific study would be impossible. It makes the scientists sad to euthanize some of the goats. But they know — many of them firsthand — that scientific research is important. Justin's son Morgan, for instance, was born prematurely. Justin knows that animal testing is important in creating lifesaving treatments for preemie babies.

Some people are against animal testing altogether. Others accept that animal lives are sometimes cut short. Scientists like Randy, Justin, and Holly try to make the animals' time on earth joyful — even if it only means a bucket to play with when they're young.

In addition, many people want to make sure that ethics, or doing what is considered to be the right thing, keeps up with breakthroughs in transgenic science. There are many ethical concerns about transgenic plants and animals.

E. coli in the Lab

IF YOUR MOM OR DAD places cooked and raw meat on separate trays, it's probably to avoid E. coli bacteria. There are actually several types of E. coli, which stands for Escherichia coli. Most are harmless. In fact, some are living peacefully inside your digestive system right now. Your parents are avoiding dangerous strains, such as E. coli O157:H7. It can lurk inside uncooked meat and unpasteurized milk. It can also spread through unwashed hands or water containing sewage. Bad E. coli can give you a stomachache or make you seriously ill. E. coli used in science labs are not harmful.

Raw meat can contain harmful strains of E. coli. Cooking the meat kills the bacteria. Raw meat and cooked meat are usually kept on separate platters so that bacteria from the raw meat doesn't contaminate the cooked meat.

TRANSGENIC ORGANISMS: ETHICAL CONCERNS AND LIFESAVING POSSIBILITIES

WALK DOWN MOST SUPERMARKET AISLES, and you'll see foods containing transgenic plants, including Roundup Ready soybeans. They're genetically modified to resist the herbicide called Roundup. When Roundup is sprayed, it kills weeds, but not soybeans. Soybean oil is found in everything from baby formula to pancake mix, and most soybeans sold in the United States are Roundup Ready. (Organic soybeans are not Roundup Ready.) Some people object to the use of Roundup Ready soybeans.

Here, we won't look at concerns about Roundup, the herbicide, which is unrelated to Randy's work with transgenic plants. Instead we'll look at people's concerns about plants being transgenic. One concern is that people might be allergic to the genetically modified plants. Randy believes this worry to be unfounded. He thinks that genetically modified plants are no more likely to cause allergies than hybrids. Hybrids result from two types of plants crossbreeding. A farmer can cause this to happen, or it can happen accidently. Either

way, it results in a new plant with a slightly different genome. Randy says that unlike hybrids, transgenic plants are tested to prove that they don't cause health problems, and that this makes them safer than hybrids. Randy thinks that transgenic plants could be raised more efficiently than regular plants. They could alleviate hunger where there are food shortages.

He says that a legitimate concern with transgenic plants is cross-pollination. Insects spread pollen from plant to plant. This allows plants from one field to crossbreed with plants in another field. (This is how hybrid plants are created.) A transgenic plant could cross-pollinate with a non-transgenic plant in a farmer's

No, these aren't spider pigs. However, they *are* transgenic. Each pig has a mouse gene. The gene allows them to digest their food better, making their manure more earth-friendly.

A common transgenic plant is the soybean. Many foods contain soybeans, and most U.S. soybeans are Roundup Ready. Transgenic crops are also referred to as genetically modified organisms, or GMOs.

ABOVE: Pollination by insects can allow transgenic crops to crossbreed with nontransgenic crops, which would be a problem for organic farmers.

Transgenic goats.

field. The result could be a new transgenic plant. The issue for organic farmers is that transgenic plants aren't classified as organic. An organic farmer would be unable to sell transgenic produce under that label. Farmers are also concerned because Monsanto, the company that makes Roundup Ready soybeans, patents their seeds. If a farmer's crops crossed with Roundup Ready soybeans, he or she could be sued for patent infringement. Family farmers have sought legal protection against this possibility.

In Europe, Africa, and Mexico many people are anti-transgenic. Randy doesn't think those feelings are as strong in America. But they do exist. Recently, organic farmers and other seed companies sought a nationwide ban on Roundup Ready alfalfa. They were concerned that organic alfalfa would cross-pollinate with Roundup Ready alfalfa. The ban has since been lifted. Randy's alfalfa would be transgenic, but not Roundup Ready.

Unlike plants, transgenic animals are not something you are likely to see every day. But they're certainly not limited to spider goats. Transgenic animals are helping scientists solve problems, develop medicines, and find lifesaving cures. Some examples:

1. GTC Biotherapeutics produces the protein antithrombin in goats' milk. One in five thousand Americans is deficient in this protein, and these people can develop deadly blood clots. Goats are implanted with human genes that tell their bodies to produce the protein in

Transgenic cancer-resistant mouse.

Transgenic GloFish®.

their milk. The protein is then given to patients in the form of medicine. As you can see, these goats are similar in some ways to the spider goats.

2. Scientists at the University of Kentucky developed a cancer-resistant mouse. They implanted the mouse with a cancer-fighting human gene called Par-4. The gene caused cancer cells—but not healthy cells—to die. A human with cancer could be implanted with the same gene through a bone marrow transplant. The gene would treat the cancer without the painful side effects that accompany radiation and chemotherapy.

3. A scientist at the National University of Singapore implanted jellyfish genes into zebra fish, causing them to glow. His next step was to engineer the fish to glow only when exposed to pollution. The zebra fish that glow regardless of pollution are now sold as pets called GloFish®.

4. Pigs have a hard time breaking down the phosphorus in their grain feed. Much of the phosphorus is passed through their digestive system. This not only makes their poop incredibly stinky, but it also causes environmental problems. Pig poop is used as fertilizer. When it rains, the fertilizer washes into the waterways. The phosphorus causes large algae blooms, which destroy aquatic ecosystems. Scientists at the University of Guelph in Ontario, Canada, implanted pigs with a mouse gene. The gene allows the pigs to break down phosphorus so that their manure contains much less phosphorus. If approved by the FDA, the pigs could

be among the first genetically modified animals to be sold as food.

Transgenic animals, plants, and bacteria are created

+ for scientific research, as is the case with the cancer-resistant mouse
+ to be resistant to disease or poison (Roundup Ready soybeans)
+ to produce something that will benefit others (the spider goats)
+ to solve a problem associated with the species itself, as is the case with the pigs

Just as transgenic plants have raised ethical concerns, so have transgenic animals. Unlike

Transgenic pigs in pen. Transgenic animals are kept separate from other animals.

plants, they pose little threat of crossbreeding. Typically, breeding is controlled by scientists. Rather, the concerns are based on how the animals are treated and how transgenic technology will be used.

Animal rights activists think that work with transgenic animals is another way of exploiting animals. The federal government regulates transgenic animals: they can be created only for medical or scientific benefit. Scientists must prove to the FDA that there will be no ill effects caused by the animals being transgenic. The USDA inspects research barns to ensure proper treatment of animals. Suffering is to be minimized. However, some studies are painful for the animals. In the case of Randy's goats, their being transgenic isn't painful. The goats

are simply milked. In fact, says Randy, because the goats are so valuable, they're pampered. If Justin and Holly's paper is accepted, the lab may be able to sell nontransgenic goats instead of euthanizing them.

Randy says that raising ethical concerns is important. One reason he welcomes television crews to the barn is to illustrate that the goats are treated well. "People *should* be concerned as to how they're treated," he says. "They're treated as well as or better than other goats. They're indistinguishable from other goats, health-wise. We have babies from babies from babies. There's no way to distinguish them from their nontransgenic counterparts."

While Randy thinks that ethical discussions are good, he objects to people condemn-

ing animal or transgenic research as a whole. He says that people, including children, rely on medical treatments developed through this research. "They [protesters] shouldn't be able to dictate what other people can have when patients don't have another option," he says.

Randy sees great possibilities in the world of transgenics. Goats could be bioengineered to produce vaccines in their milk. This would solve a problem encountered in some third world countries. Vaccines must be frozen. Many towns don't have cold storage. The vaccine would stay fresh in the goats' milk. Children would drink the milk and be immunized. "You just milk the goats and feed the kids," Randy says. "In this case, the human kids, not the goat kids."

On the science side, some people think that transgenic technology will be misused. They worry that if human genes can be altered, it will lead to "designer babies," babies altered to grow up stronger, faster, or more beautiful. Scientists *do* want to genetically alter humans, but in a different way. Scientists are researching ways to alter genes so that children aren't born with fatal genetic diseases such as cystic fibrosis or sickle cell anemia. Randy says that some of the concerns about genetic research miss the mark. "It's not going to lead to designer babies," he says. "It's going to lead to babies not being born with diseases."

Some people object to transgenic plants and animals because they think that it's like "playing God." They don't think the genetic makeup of things should be tampered with. The flip side of this argument is this: If humans are given tools, through nature and scientific progress, to cure diseases and improve lives, are we not ethically obligated to use them? It's one thing to be unaware of a cure for a spinal cord injury. In that case, no one would expect you to heal that injury. But what if you knew how to cure it? Would you be obligated to help? Scientists don't know if bioengineered spider silk could be used in such a scenario. But they want to find out.

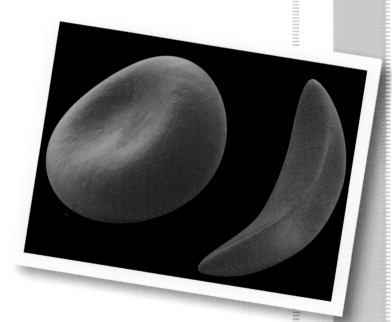

Sickle cell anemia is a genetic disease. It causes a person's blood cells to be sickle shaped instead of round. The sickle cells cling to artery walls, resulting in poor circulation. The disease makes sufferers feel sick and fatigued, and it can lead to premature death.

Be a Part of the Discussion

Do YOU THINK transgenic plants and animals can help people?

Do you think transgenic plants and animals should be allowed?

Do you think animal testing should be allowed? What rules do you think animal testing should follow?

SPINNING SPIDER SILK

You've seen spider goats and spider alfalfa. Now it's time to see spider silk as a fiber — like cotton. You could wear a shirt made of spider silk. It would be spun into thread, woven into cloth, and then sewn into a shirt. Spider silk clothing is probably a few years away. For now, Randy's team spins spider silk to test its properties.

The spinning machine, in a lab room down the hall, is similar to those that spin nylon, polyester, and even Kevlar (though Kevlar is melted before being spun). Randy, Justin, and Mike Hinman prepare to spin spider silk. Spider silk protein powder (from goats' milk) has been put into liquid chemicals. This is called spindope.

Randy and Justin monitor the hydraulics. Hydraulics push the dope through a syringe and into isopropyl alcohol (also known as rubbing alcohol), which removes the solvent. Now the spider silk is a fiber. Mike waits with tweezers. A longtime research scientist, he has bioengineered spider silk genes and, along with

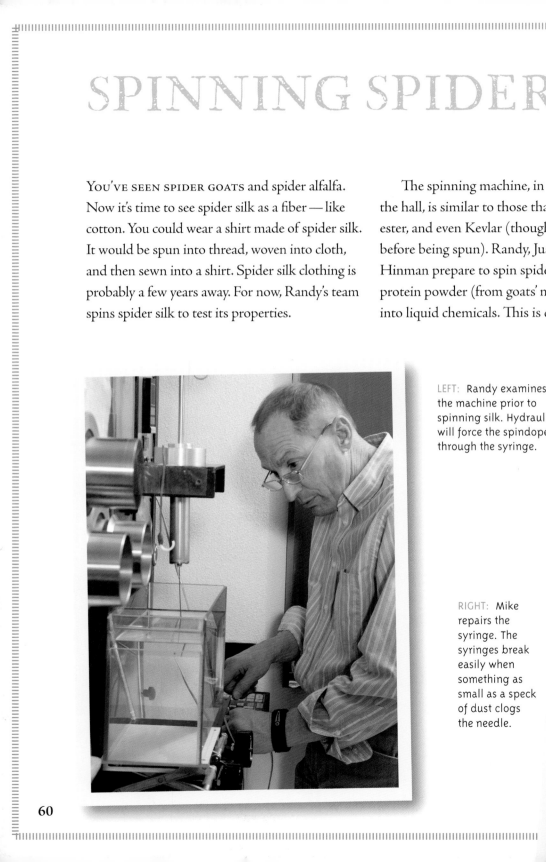

LEFT: Randy examines the machine prior to spinning silk. Hydraulics will force the spindope through the syringe.

RIGHT: Mike repairs the syringe. The syringes break easily when something as small as a speck of dust clogs the needle.

Flo Teulé, is the resident expert on spinning spider silk.

With tweezers he lifts the silk out of the rubbing alcohol and guides it over a hook and onto a godet, pronounced *go-day*. The godet, an innovation of the fabric industry, is made up of two spools that spin at variable speeds. The fiber stretches as it wraps around the spools. This process lines up proteins and reinforces structure, making the fiber tougher.

That is, Mike *tries* to guide the silk onto the godet. Spinning spider silk is tricky. A speck of dust in the test tube causes the dope to clog the needle and emerge as a blob. If the blob meets

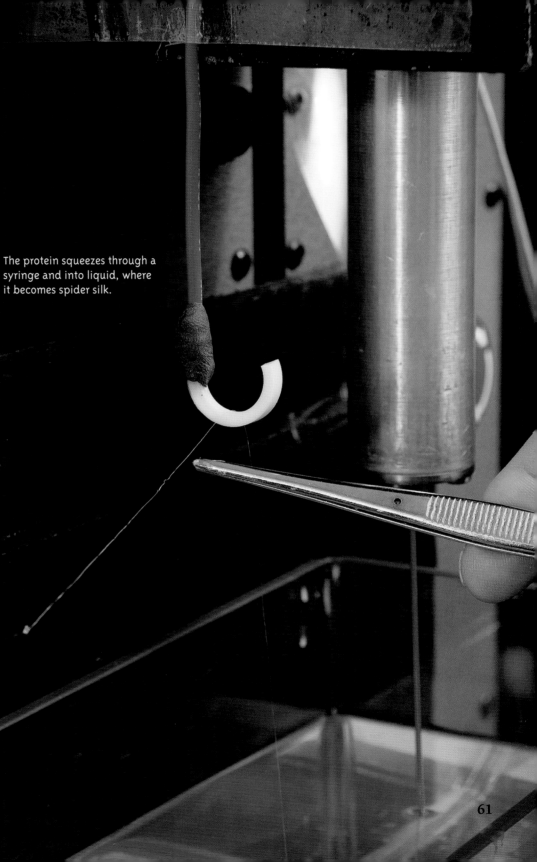

The protein squeezes through a syringe and into liquid, where it becomes spider silk.

At first, the spider silk proteins are dissolved in chemicals. This is called spindope.

Spider silk gathers around the spool. It is opaque or clear, unlike the golden native silk.

The stress-strain machine tests the strength and flexibility of spider silk by pulling a strand in either direction.

any resistance, it breaks. Even without a blob the spider silk easily snags. Mike tweezes the silk so that it doesn't catch on his fingertips. When the silk snags, it breaks. Yes, spider silk is strong. But even the strongest fiber is fragile when its diameter is one-fifth that of a human hair. This spider silk sample keeps snagging and breaking. Silk floats around Mike and sticks to him. He says, "This is how we end up festooned with spider silk webs — it's like walking through the woods." Eventually it becomes clear that it can't be spun.

On the second try, Mike spins spider silk proteins made by bacteria. This time the spinning goes smoothly and the silk winds onto the spool. When things go well, Mike can gather about five meters of silk. But even a few inches (about eight centimeters) are enough for testing. A machine performs a stress-strain test. The machine pulls the strand of silk up. Randy explains that stress is the force applied to the silk before it breaks. Strain is the percent of its original length that the silk is able to stretch before breaking. Together, stress and strain determine toughness.

Randy's team works constantly to create the toughest silk. In addition to bioengineering an array of spider silk genes,

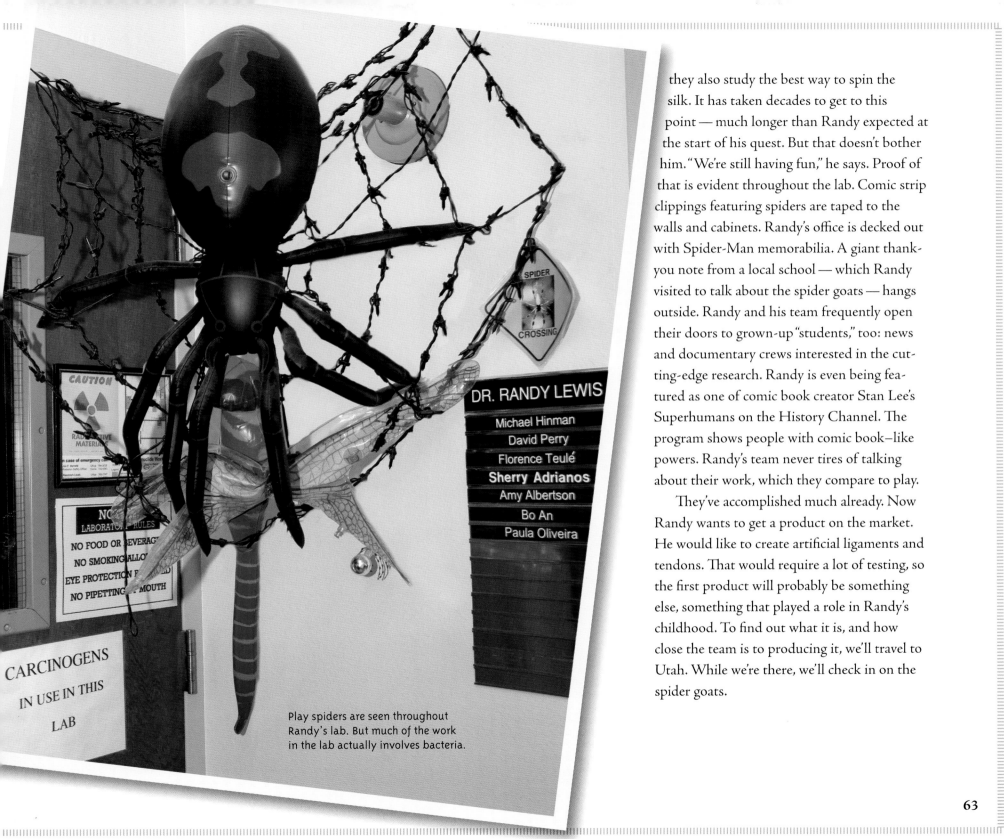

CAUTION

RADIOACTIVE MATERIAL

NO
LABORATORY RULES

NO FOOD OR BEVERAG
NO SMOKING ALLO
EYE PROTECTION P
NO PIPETTING MOUTH

CARCINOGENS
IN USE IN THIS
LAB

SPIDER
CROSSING

DR. RANDY LEWIS

Michael Hinman
David Perry
Florence Teulé
Sherry Adrianos
Amy Albertson
Bo An
Paula Oliveira

Play spiders are seen throughout Randy's lab. But much of the work in the lab actually involves bacteria.

they also study the best way to spin the silk. It has taken decades to get to this point — much longer than Randy expected at the start of his quest. But that doesn't bother him. "We're still having fun," he says. Proof of that is evident throughout the lab. Comic strip clippings featuring spiders are taped to the walls and cabinets. Randy's office is decked out with Spider-Man memorabilia. A giant thank-you note from a local school — which Randy visited to talk about the spider goats — hangs outside. Randy and his team frequently open their doors to grown-up "students," too: news and documentary crews interested in the cutting-edge research. Randy is even being featured as one of comic book creator Stan Lee's Superhumans on the History Channel. The program shows people with comic book–like powers. Randy's team never tires of talking about their work, which they compare to play.

They've accomplished much already. Now Randy wants to get a product on the market. He would like to create artificial ligaments and tendons. That would require a lot of testing, so the first product will probably be something else, something that played a role in Randy's childhood. To find out what it is, and how close the team is to producing it, we'll travel to Utah. While we're there, we'll check in on the spider goats.

A NEW LAB: UTAH

In the Spring of 2011 Randy and his team blaze a trail across the mountains — machines and goats in tow. They arrive at Utah State University, which is nestled in a valley along the western edge of the Rockies. They join the USTAR program, which recruits cutting-edge scientists to build the state's technology industry. Mike, Justin, and Flo remain part of the team. Holly and Heather stay at the University of Wyoming. Sherry moves to Kansas State. They'll all continue their work in science. In Utah, several bioengineering students join Randy's team. They're studying how to make transgenic organisms and how to produce products from transgenic organisms.

When we walk into the new lab, progress is immediately apparent. Inside the lypholyzer (a freeze-dry machine that is the final step in spider silk protein purification) there is visibly more spider silk protein than we saw in the Wyoming lab. Randy confirms that more protein is being produced here at Utah State.

Justin introduces us to one of the undergrads working on the TFF (the milk filtration machine). Howard Cordingley, a bioengineering student, says that with Heather's streamlined process, more workers (including Howard

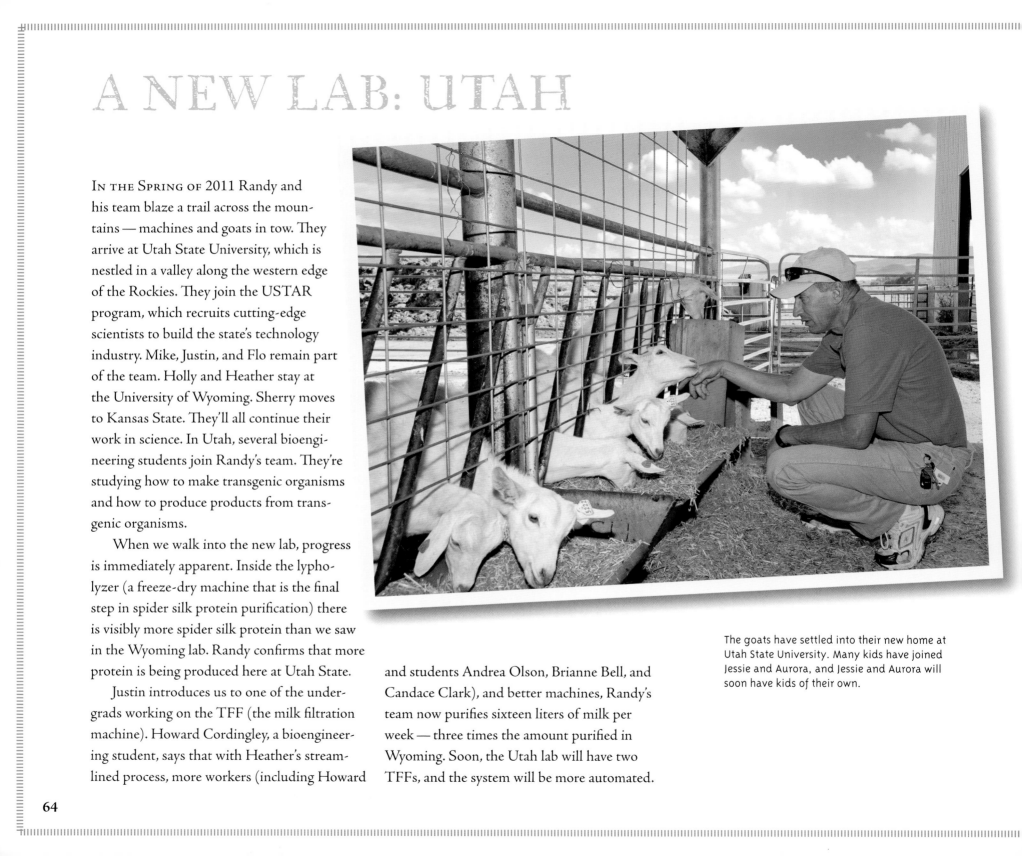

The goats have settled into their new home at Utah State University. Many kids have joined Jessie and Aurora, and Jessie and Aurora will soon have kids of their own.

and students Andrea Olson, Brianne Bell, and Candace Clark), and better machines, Randy's team now purifies sixteen liters of milk per week — three times the amount purified in Wyoming. Soon, the Utah lab will have two TFFs, and the system will be more automated.

At that point the amount of purified milk will more than double. That's good because, as in Wyoming, the goats produce a lot of milk, four hundred liters in the past six months alone.

Andy and I are eager to see the spider goats in their new home. Here in Utah the goats share one facility but live in separate pens. We see some familiar faces. In the billy pen, Frankie, the goat formerly known as GQ, and Tap, another one of the smaller billies from Wyoming, approach us. Uzi, the big daddy, lazes about in the hay. Randy tells us that Chewy, the transgenic father of many kids, passed away in Wyoming. He introduces us to a new billy, King Kong. He was born a single kid, which is somewhat unusual. He was bigger than the other kids and liked to throw his weight around. When he climbed onto the bucket, he wouldn't let anybody else up on it. Randy thought such a big, powerful goat would benefit the herd. He kept King Kong as a new transgenic billy.

When King Kong first joined the billies, he butted heads with them. That didn't work. "They thumped him," Randy says. King Kong learned that though he was the biggest kid, he was the smallest billy. Now he hangs out in his own corner, knowing his place, or perhaps biding his time.

Beside the billies are the kids. In May, eleven transgenic females were born. The two January kids, Jessie and Aurora, also reside in the kid pen. They're as playful as ever. A curious Jes-

RIGHT: Howard Cordingley and Andrea Olson check the new tangential flow filtration (TFF) machine as it purifies milk. Three times as much spider milk is being purified each day since the move to Utah State.

A new billy goat, King Kong, has joined the herd. He was a towering beast among the other kids, but in the male pen he is the smallest.

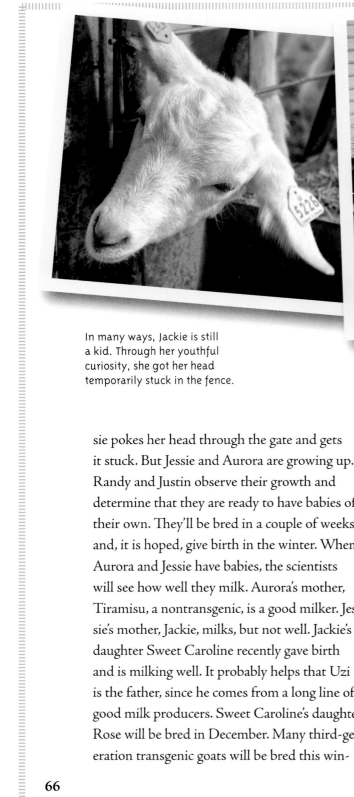

In many ways, Jackie is still a kid. Through her youthful curiosity, she got her head temporarily stuck in the fence.

Justin and Randy take stock of which of the does are old enough to be bred.

Twins Baby and Princess are part of Justin and Holly's paper showing that a spider gene from a transgenic goat is not transferred to a nontransgenic goat in utero.

sie pokes her head through the gate and gets it stuck. But Jessie and Aurora are growing up. Randy and Justin observe their growth and determine that they are ready to have babies of their own. They'll be bred in a couple of weeks, and, it is hoped, give birth in the winter. When Aurora and Jessie have babies, the scientists will see how well they milk. Aurora's mother, Tiramisu, a nontransgenic, is a good milker. Jessie's mother, Jackie, milks, but not well. Jackie's daughter Sweet Caroline recently gave birth and is milking well. It probably helps that Uzi is the father, since he comes from a long line of good milk producers. Sweet Caroline's daughter Rose will be bred in December. Many third-generation transgenic goats will be bred this win-

ter, and their milk production will be watched closely.

Randy says that breed standards are for a goat to produce four to six liters per day. Some of the transgenic goats produce only about a liter. The goal is for each liter to have more than a gram of spider silk protein in it. Some does produce more than that. Jackie and Daisy, for instance, produce three grams per liter. Randy is concerned more with the milk production than with the amount of protein. "Getting them to produce more milk is the top priority," he says. "Silk production will follow."

If the goats milk poorly, it could be because they're poor milkers in general or they're poor milkers with the spider silk protein. Randy

wants to breed goats that are good milkers *with* the spider silk protein.

Freckles remains one of the best milkers. In the does' pen, she approaches Justin, as friendly as ever. She seems to pose for the camera. She gave birth to twins again in May. Her daughter Lovey passed away, but Squidget, so named for her tininess at birth, is thriving. "Squidget was tiny," Randy said. "She made up for it by getting big around." Her trick is to jump into the trough. She slips and falls and then stands there for the better part of the day. Two of Freckles's older daughters, Princess and Baby, will be bred for the first time in a couple of weeks. Only Princess is transgenic. The twins were part of the study conducted by Justin and

Doctoral student Michaela Hugie cuts alfalfa leaves to test them for the spider silk protein.

Holly to show that a transgenic baby does not pass transgenic genes to a nontransgenic twin in utero.

Justin and Holly have received good news: Their paper based on this study was accepted. Soon, the lab may be able to sell all non-transgenic goats. They will live on, likely as dairy goats.

In addition to the third-generation goats from the original herd set to breed in the fall, a new herd will soon be implanted with new genes. These will probably be genes that Flo designed. Randy says they tested well in the bacteria and did well in the transgenic silkworms. Each goat will get one of four genes. The largest is the same or nearly the same size as genes in actual spiders. Larger genes will result in larger proteins. Larger

proteins will probably result in stronger silk. The silk Randy's lab is making is already stretchy enough, so that's not a factor.

Randy theorizes that larger proteins make stronger silk because the fiber has fewer weak spots. At the end of each protein, the molecules are not as close together. The fibers are weak at these points. Fibers with smaller proteins have more weak spots. Think of a Hershey's chocolate bar. It's divided into small rectangular sections. The bar is weakest between these sections. That way, you can break off individual sections to eat. Imagine if a bar didn't have smaller sections. It would be harder to break. You want the Hershey's bar to break. It's more fun to eat it that way. Randy doesn't want the spider silk to break, so having smaller proteins with weak spots between them is bad.

The goats are the x-factor. Will they successfully produce milk that contains the larger proteins? The silkworms received the large genes and successfully produced large proteins. Randy hopes that the goats will, too. He also hopes that the current herd will still be useful. That will

depend on whether the next generation produces more milk — and more spider silk protein in that milk.

Meanwhile, Flo revised her silkworm paper and it was accepted for publication in a peer-reviewed journal, an important step to the research process. Often, a paper must be published before work continues. This means that the Lewis lab and their collaborators will investigate whether silkworms are capable of spinning pure spider silk.

Bacteria production is scaling up, too — from thirteen liters to one hundred liters per week. A new AKTA, the machine that purifies the bacteria to get at the spider silk, is more efficient. Randy's team will try to engineer bacteria that can produce large proteins. In that case, bacteria could be used to produce spider silk for products, not just for testing.

The spider alfalfa is also making good progress. Just outside the lab, alfalfa soaks up the Utah sunshine that is streaming through the window. In Wyoming, Holly determined these plants to be spider alfalfa. Now, in Utah, doctoral student Michaela Hugie cuts leaves and stores them in plastic bags. When she has ten grams of leaves from each plant, she'll test which plants produce spider silk proteins. Michaela will grow new plants from cuttings. She is studying how Randy's lab can scale up alfalfa production. Eventually, fields of alfalfa could produce a great deal of spider silk protein. She says they hope to scale up in several months to a year.

Spider . . . Cotton?

THERE MAY BE another "spider plant." Randy is testing whether cotton could be made to produce spider silk proteins. Interestingly, the spider silk proteins would not be in the cotton bolls, which are mostly carbohydrate. They wouldn't be efficient at producing a protein. Instead, they'd be produced in the seed. The seed could produce spider silk protein, and the cotton could still be used for clothing.

Cotton balls.

All My Kids

THE GOAT FAMILY TREES are as intertwined as characters on *All My Children*. Here are a few family sagas that the scientists are watching closely. They want to know whether the babies of Freckles, Jackie, and Tiramisu will grow up to produce more milk than their mothers.

TIRAMISU (NONTRANSGENIC) + CHEWY (TRANSGENIC, DECEASED)

AURORA

Aurora will be bred soon. Will Tiramisu's transgenic daughter milk as well as Tiramisu does? And will Aurora's offspring live up to their mom's reputation of being the best-looking goat in the herd?

FRECKLES (TRANSGENIC) + UZI (NONTRANSGENIC)

JACKIE (TRANSGENIC) + UZI (NONTRANSGENIC)

SQUIDGET PRINCESS BABY

JESSIE SWEET CAROLINE

ROSE

Lovey and Squidget were born this spring. Lovey died, and Squidget was born small, but she is now doing well. Squidget's older twin sisters, transgenic Princess and nontransgenic Baby, will be bred in a couple of weeks for the first time. Will these three daughters be star milkers like Freckles?

Jessie will be bred in a couple of weeks. She is just seven months old, but that is standard breeding age for goats. Big sister Sweet Caroline gave birth to Rose in the spring. Jackie's granddaughter will breed in December. Will the transgenic girls milk better than their transgenic mother?

HAVE YOU GUESSED WHAT THE FIRST SPIDER SILK PRODUCT WILL BE?

BELOW: Mike continues to design spider silk genes and study the best way to spin silk. He hopes to create bioengineered silk strong enough to hold this Spider-Man action figure.

RANDY KNOWS that it is not only proteins that make spider silk tough — it's how the fiber is spun. In Utah, Randy's team hopes to find the best way to spin spider silk. Spiders spin silk perfectly. Liquid proteins from their silk ducts squeeze through the spinnerets (which are shaped like tubes) as the spider pulls away. Now, it's silk. Randy's team wants to imitate this process.

Doctorate student Cameron Copeland is studying how liquid, heat, and speed play a role. He's placed a tray under the godet, which will contain a liquid mixture of water, isopropanol, and salt. The silk will run through the liquid before stretching on the godet. Cameron will also test whether heating the liquid makes the silk tougher. Finally, he will test the speed at which the silk is stretched. "We're confident enough to make the fiber," he says. "Now we want to make the fiber as good as possible."

Mike Hinman continues to work toward a stronger fiber as well, by both bioengineering new genes and working on the spinning process. In his office in Utah, he has a Spider-Man action figure. One of his goals is for his bioengineered silk to bear the weight of that Spider-Man.

Once the spinning process is perfected, a larger, more automated machine will mass-produce the silk. At that point several spider silk products may enter the marketplace. The scientists smile when asked which product they're most excited about. To see their hard work result in a helpful or even lifesaving product will be a dream come true.

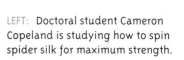

LEFT: Doctoral student Cameron Copeland is studying how to spin spider silk for maximum strength.

Randy can now fly fish in a stream running through his and Lorrie's backyard in Logan, Utah.

Howard Cordingley

Andrea Olson

Michaela Hugie

Howard, Andrea, and Michaela are most excited about a spider silk bulletproof vest. Howard, a veteran of the Iraq War, says, "Wearing a Kevlar vest in 120-degree [F] heat is no fun." Transporting the heavy vests is also a problem. "Instead of carrying the weight of the vests, you could carry water," he says.

For Mike, an obvious choice might be a bioengineered tendon or ligament, as he has a chronic foot injury. But he chooses a more romantic option: a space suit. Spider silk can freeze to negative eighty degrees Celcius (-112°F) and retain its flexibility, so it may endure the coldness of space, he says.

Many of the scientists are most excited about the medical applications for spider silk. Justin looks forward to a ligament or tendon product or a product that helps with bone regeneration. He also thinks car airbags would be exciting. Flo would like to see spider silk help the injured. One use she's especially interested in is wound dressing for burn victims.

Cameron and Brianne are excited about tendon and ligament repair. Cameron injured his ankle playing basketball as a kid. It healed through rest — but not completely. Spider silk could be used as an artificial ligament or to create structure while a tendon healed.

Randy hopes that his son will one day help surgical patients by using spider silk products. Two to five years of animal testing will be required to ensure safety. So far, animals exposed to spider silk have had no allergic reactions. But scientists also have to test whether spider silk's mechanical properties can hold up in the body. That is, would artificial ligaments and tendons remain tough? Would sutures hold up? Randy has time for his dream to come to fruition. "[Brian will] be doing surgery for a long time," Randy says. "That gives me quite a window to get it there."

In the meantime, a nonmedical product will probably hit the market first. It's something that would have interested Randy's father: a fly tippet. That's the fiber that ties the hook (complete with the fly lure) to the fishing line. Spider silk would be stronger but thinner than the man-made fiber currently on the market. The fish would be less likely to see it, bite through it, or break it by tugging on the line.

Randy has been a fly-fisherman since he

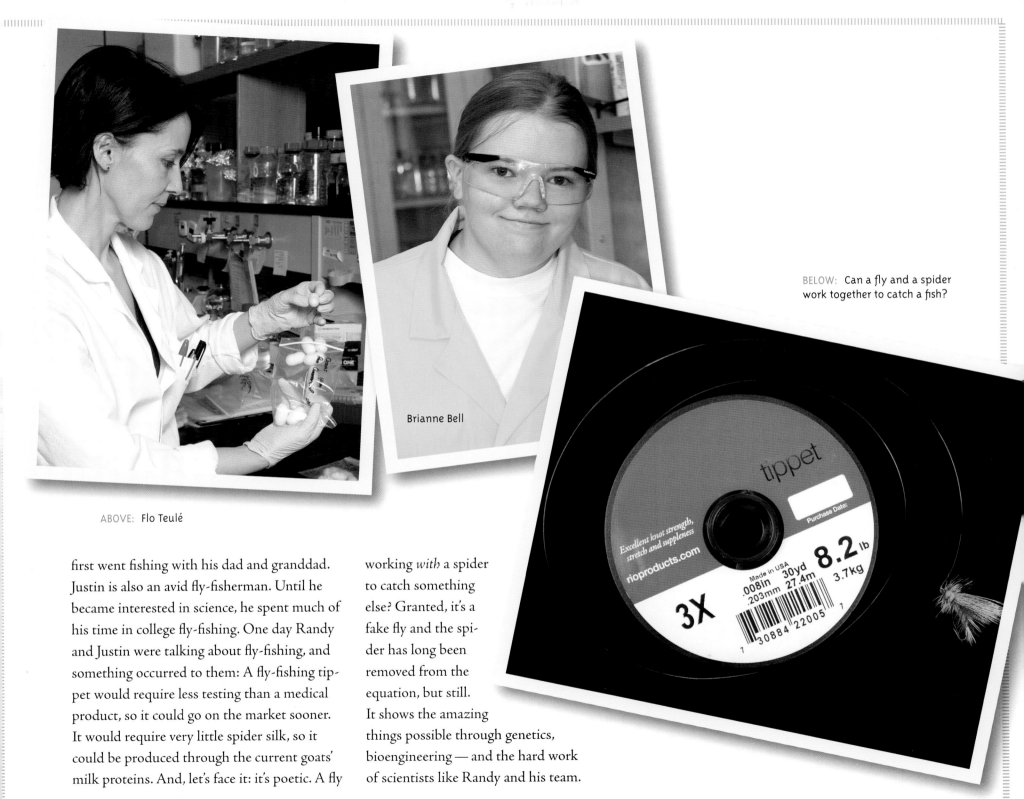

ABOVE: Flo Teulé

Brianne Bell

BELOW: Can a fly and a spider work together to catch a fish?

tippet

Excellent knot strength, stretch and suppleness
rioproducts.com

Made in USA
.008in 30yd
.203mm 27.4m

8.2 lb
3.7kg

3X

7 30884 22005 7

first went fishing with his dad and granddad. Justin is also an avid fly-fisherman. Until he became interested in science, he spent much of his time in college fly-fishing. One day Randy and Justin were talking about fly-fishing, and something occurred to them: A fly-fishing tippet would require less testing than a medical product, so it could go on the market sooner. It would require very little spider silk, so it could be produced through the current goats' milk proteins. And, let's face it: it's poetic. A fly working *with* a spider to catch something else? Granted, it's a fake fly and the spider has long been removed from the equation, but still. It shows the amazing things possible through genetics, bioengineering — and the hard work of scientists like Randy and his team.

Space Spiders

WHILE WE WERE IN UTAH, Randy's lab was working on a NASA project involving spider astronauts. Two golden orb weavers, Esmeralda and Gladys, had rocketed onboard space shuttle *Endeavor* to the International Space Station (in separate containers, of course). There, scientists observed how they spun their webs in the microgravity of space. Microgravity means weak gravity. It's why astronauts float when they are in the space station.

Upon the spiders' return to earth, some of the silk was sent to Randy's lab. Randy's team tested whether the silk's mechanical properties were different from usual. Cameron teased a silk strand from the tangled web. Then he tested it on the stress-strain machine. This would be good practice for when he spun silk for his thesis. His tests showed that the space spider silk had the same mechanical properties as regular spider silk. Microgravity had no effect on the spider silk fibers.

The spiders aren't the only invertebrates that have lifted off. NASA has also brought butterflies, worms, and fruit flies into space to examine how microgravity affects them. During this trip, the fruit flies were studied by scientists but also eaten by Gladys and Esmeralda.

Space Shuttle Endeavor launched May 18, 2011, headed for the International Space Station. In addition to six human astronauts, two spider astronauts were on board.

Will space spider silk be different from earthly spider silk? Cameron prepares silk for testing on the stress-strain machine.

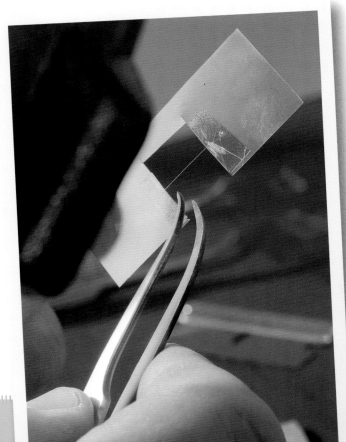

LEFT AND ABOVE: Cameron untangles
silk from the space spiders.

Glossary

agrobacteria Bacteria that infect plants.

allele A variant in a gene that tends to run in families.

amino acids The twenty (plus five very rare) acids that link together to form proteins.

arachnid An invertebrate that usually has eight legs, no antennae, and simple eyes, and that lives on land. Examples include spiders, mites, and scorpions.

bacteria Simple organisms, usually single-celled, without chlorophyll.

bioengineering Making products through biological systems, such as changing plants and animals genetically to derive a protein.

callus Undifferentiated cells in plants.

casein One of the main proteins in milk.

cell A unit that makes up all living things. It usually contains a nucleus, cytoplasm, and a membrane.

cocoon A protective home that some caterpillars spin (of silk) in order to metamorphose inside of it.

curds The solid components that result from milk being processed. They are used in cheesemaking.

cytoplasm The area of the cell outside the nucleus.

DNA Deoxyribonucleic acid. The instructions for building proteins and other life systems.

E. coli *Escherichia coli*. A species of bacteria present in the intestines of humans and other animals and used in biological research. Some strains cause sickness.

fiber A substance that can be spun as a thread, or a threadlike structure that occurs in nature and makes up tissue, such as muscle.

gene The set of instructions, written in DNA, for building a protein.

genetics The study of genes, genomes, and heredity.

genome The complete set of genes and other DNA for any given organism or species.

keratin The main protein in hair, nails, and horns.

molecular biology The study of molecules in living cells.

mRNA Messenger ribonucleic acid. A copy of DNA, read by ribosomes as instructions for building proteins.

native silk Silk spun by a spider, as opposed to being genetically engineered.

nucleus The central part of a cell, containing an organism's genome.

protein A substance composed of amino acids and largely responsible for the structure and functions of living things.

purify To remove all but the desired substance.

ribosomes Particles, made of RNA and proteins, that read mRNA and use the instructions to build a protein.

sericin A gluelike substance produced by silkworms to coat silk and hold the cocoon together.

silk A threadlike fiber produced by living things, such as silkworms or spiders.

spider An arachnid that spins silk through spinnerets.

spinneret The organ in spiders and caterpillars through which liquid silk is pushed to become solid silk.

transgenic An organism containing one or more genes from another species.

whey The liquid part of milk after the curds are separated.

wild-type Not transgenic.

Acknowledgments

BRIDGET AND ANDY would like to thank Randy Lewis, his wife, Lorrie Lewis, his sister Cindy Lewis, and the teams at the University of Wyoming and Utah State University. Randy, along with research scientists Florence Teulé, Justin Jones, Mike Hinman, Heather Rothfuss, Holly Steinkraus, and Don Jarvis; doctoral students Sherry Adrianos, Cameron Copeland, Michaela Hugie, and Bo An; and undergrads Howard Cordingley, Andrea Olson, Candace Clark, and Brianne Bell were unbelievably generous with their time, knowledge, and patience as they explained the process of creating spider goats, spider alfalfa, spider silkworms, and spider bacteria. Randy opened his lab to us, as he has to many television, documentary, and news crews, in order to share the amazing progress and possibilities in the field of genetics. A special thank-you to Dr. Brian Matsumoto, as well.

In addition, we'd like to thank Andrew and Morgan Jones for sharing their goat play expertise, and Zane Rothfuss and Morgan for letting spiders crawl on them in the name of science. And, if they're reading this, we'd like to thank the goats, spiders, silkworms, sheep, and bacteria, even the stinky kind. What's that? Oh, yes, of course. Alfalfa, we'd like to thank you, too.

Finally, thank you to editors Erica Zappy and Cynthia Platt, copyeditor Maxine Bartow, and the entire team at Houghton Mifflin for bringing this book together. Bridget would like to thank the photographer Andy Comins for his amazing work, her agent Kelly Sonnack, and her family.

Nephila clavipes, golden orb weaver, drinking water droplets.

All My Kids Update:

Aurora gave birth to a baby billy. Her milk is high in spider silk protein. Jessie is expecting her first kid.

Additional Sources

Anquetil, Jacques. *Silk*. Photos by Marc Walter. Paris: Flammarion, 1995.

Bald, Lisa. "Billboard Pits Child vs. Rat." *NBC Chicago*. April 28, 2011.

Biomedical Research. The Humane Society of the United States website. www.humanesociety.org/issues/ biomedical_research.

Braiker, Brian. "'Enviropig'…or Frankenswine?" *ABC News*. January 6, 2011. abcnews.go.com/Technology/enviropig- ontario-canada-university-guelph-geneti- cally-engineered-pigs/story?id=12555908.

Drew, Amy. "The Wide Angle: Top 10 Eccen- tric Transgenic Animals." *Discovery Tech*. dsc.discovery.com/technology/ tech-10/genetic-engineering/ 10-transgenic-animals.html.

National University of Singapore. "Zebra Fish as Pollution Indicators." www.nus.edu.sg/research/rg12.php

Pollack, Andrew. "F.D.A. Approves Drug from Gene-Altered Goats." *New York Times*. Feb- ruary 6, 2009. www.nytimes.com/2009/02/07/ business/07goatdrug.html.

Rolph, Amy. "PETA Targets UW with 'Murder' Billboards." *Seattle Pi. Seattle's Big Blog*. June 15, 2011. blog.seattlepi.com/thebigblog/ 2011/06/15/peta-targets-uw-with- murder-billboards.

Schoeser, Mary. *Silk*. Foreword by Julien Macdonald. New Haven, Conn.: Yale University Press, 2007.

Schurman, Rachel. *Fighting for the Future of Food: Activists Versus Agribusiness in the Struggle over Biotechnology*. Minneapolis: University of Minnesota Press, 2010.

University of Kentucky. "UK Creates Cancer- Resistant Mouse." November 27, 2007. news.uky.edu/news/display_article. php?artid=2937.

Vernon, Jamie. "PETA Should Rethink Its Campaign Against Animal Research." *The Intersection. Discover Magazine Blogs*. June 30, 2011. blogs.discovermagazine.com/ intersection/2011/06/30/peta-should- rethink-its-campaign-against-animal- research.

Index

SCIENTISTS IN THE FIELD
Where Science Meets Adventure

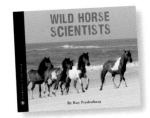

Check out these titles to meet more scientists who are out in the field—and contributing every day to our knowledge of the world around us:

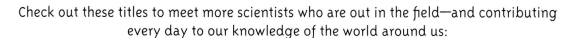

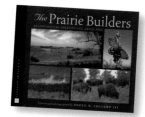

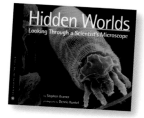
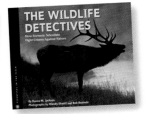

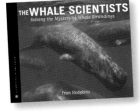

Looking for even more adventure? Craving updates on the work of your favorite scientists, as well as in-depth video footage, audio, photography, and more? Then visit the new Scientists in the Field website!

www.sciencemeetsadventure.com